The Père Marquette
Lecture in Theology
2010

SONG AND MEMORY

BIBLICAL WOMEN

IN SYRIAC TRADITION

by

SUSAN ASHBROOK HARVEY

MARQUETTE
UNIVERSITY
PRESS

LIBRARY OF CONGRESS CATALOGING-IN-PUBLICATION DATA

Harvey, Susan Ashbrook.
  Song and memory : biblical women in Syriac tradition / by
Susan Ashbrook Harvey.
    p. cm. — (The Père Marquette lecture in theology ; 2010)
  Includes bibliographical references.
  ISBN-13: 978-0-87462-590-5 (hardcover : alk. paper)
  ISBN-10: 0-87462-590-4 (hardcover : alk. paper)
  1. Women in the Bible. 2. Women in Christianity. 3. Church
music—Syrian Orthodox Church. 4. Syrian Orthodox Church.
I. Title.
  BS680.W7H38 2010
  220.8'305408828163—dc22

                                                    2010006914

© 2010
Marquette University Press
Milwaukee WI 53201-3141
All rights reserved.
Manufactured in the United States of America

FOUNDED 1916

♾The paper used in this publication meets the minimum requirements of the
American National Standard for Information Sciences—
Permanence of Paper for Printed Library Materials, ANSI Z39.48-1992.

Association of American
University Presses

MARQUETTE UNIVERSITY PRESS
MILWAUKEE

The Association of Jesuit University Presses

FOREWORD

The 2010 Père Marquette Lecture in Theology is the forty-first in a series commemorating the missions and explorations of Père Jacques Marquette, SJ (1637-75). This series of lectures was begun in 1969 under the auspices of the Marquette University Department of Theology.

The Joseph A. Auchter Family Endowment Fund has endowed the lecture series. Joseph Auchter (1894-1986), a native of Milwaukee, was a banking and paper industry executive and a long-time supporter of education. The fund was established by his children as a memorial to him.

SUSAN ASHBROOK HARVEY

Susan Ashbrook Harvey is the Willard Prescott and Annie McClelland Smith Professor of Religious

Studies at Brown University. She received her BA degree in Classics from Grinnell College in Iowa, and her MLitt and PhD degrees from the University of Birmingham, England, in Byzantine History. She specializes in Syriac studies, early Christian history, and Christianity of the Byzantine and Syriac traditions. She taught at the University of North Carolina at Greensboro and at the University of Rochester before moving to Brown University in 1987.

Several areas of interest have dominated Prof. Harvey's work. She has long had a profound love for the cult of saints, early monasticism, hagiography, and especially Syriac ascetic traditions. From these interests came her first two books, *Asceticism and Society in Crisis: John of Ephesus and the Lives of the Eastern Saints* (1990); and, co-authored with Sebastian P. Brock, *Holy Women of the Syrian Orient* (1998, 1987). Her awareness of the intensely beautiful sensory imagery that characterizes Syriac hagiography led to her work on religion and the senses. This culminated in her study of smell as a category of religious experience in ancient Christianity across the Mediterranean world, *Scenting Salvation: Ancient Christianity and the Olfactory Imagination* (2006). With attention to the larger spectrum of early Christianity, she co-edited with David G. Hunter *The Oxford Handbook of Early Christian Studies* (2008). From the very start, however, she has worked on women in early Christianity, and especially in women in Syriac Christianity. In recent years, she has focused particularly on the presentation of biblical women in early Syriac hymns and verse homilies, and on the women's choirs that sang about them. She is hoping to bring her work on this material into another book soon. At the same time, she is also engaged in a new collaborative project with a group of scholars from the United States, Israel, and the Netherlands, looking at comparative Jewish and Christian liturgical poetry in late antiquity. The group is working with texts in Hebrew, Aramaic, Syriac, Greek, and Latin.

In addition to her academic obligations, Dr. Harvey serves on the Eastern Orthodox – Roman Catholic Bilateral Theological Consultation for North America.

Robert M. Doran, SJ

SONG AND MEMORY: BIBLICAL WOMEN IN SYRIAC TRADITION

BY

SUSAN ASHBROOK HARVEY

The women of the Bible left indelible memories of songs within their stories: Miriam the sister of Moses singing in celebration as she led the Hebrew women in dance at the Red Sea (Ex 15:20-21), Hannah's joyful prayer of thanksgiving at the birth of the prophet Samuel (1 Sam 2:1-10); and most loved by Christians, Mary's Magnificat, sung at her visitation to her cousin Elizabeth, during their pregnancies with Jesus and John the Baptist (Lk 1:46-55). Perhaps uniquely among the ancient Christian traditions, Syriac Christians honored this memory of women's song in the Bible. They did so in the hymns and verse homilies sung and chanted in their liturgies, into which they set the words they imagined biblical women had said. They did so again through the strong presence of women's voices in their midst, for Syriac churches cultivated a tradition of women's choirs to sing these hymns that gave musical embodiment to the women of biblical lore. With real voices and imagined words, ancient Syriac Christianity paid homage not only to the men, but also to the women whose stories comprised their sacred scriptures. My task here is to consider this striking homage: its forms, methods, purposes, and implications for our understanding of ancient Christianity.[1]

---

1   I use the following abbreviations in this essay:

Brock, *Bride of Light* = Sebastian P. Brock, *Bride of Light: Hymns on Mary from the Syriac Churches*, Moran 'Eth'o 6 (Kerala: St. Ephrem Ecumenical Research Institute, 1994).

CSCO = Corpus Scriptorum Christianorum Orientalium.

Ephrem, *Comm Gen* = Ephrem, *Commentary on Genesis*. Syriac ed. R. M. Tonneau, *Sancti Ephraem Syri in Genesim et in Exodum Commentarii*, CSCO 152 (Louvain, 1955), 3-121. English trans. Joseph P. Amar and Edward P. Matthews, Jr., *St. Ephrem the Syrian: Selected Prose Works*, Fathers of the Church 91 (Washington, DC: Catholic University of America Press, 1994), 67-220.

Ephrem, *Comm Diat* = *Saint Ephrem's Commentary on Tatian's Diatessaron*, trans. Carmel McCarthy, *Journal of Semitic Studies* Supplement 2 (Oxford: Oxford University Press for the University of Manchester, 1993).

Ephrem, *HNat* = Ephrem, *Hymns on the Nativity*. Syriac ed. Edmund Beck, *Des heiligen Ephraem des Syrers Hymnen De Nativitate (Epiphania)*, CSCO 186-87/ Scr. Syr. 82-83 (Louvain 1959); English trans. Kathleen McVey, *Ephrem the Syrian: Hymns* (New York: Paulist Press, 1989), 61-218.

I. THE SYRIAC CONTEXT

Syriac is a dialect of Aramaic, itself a dialect of Hebrew. It emerged in the eastern Mediterranean during the early Christian period. Originally a dialect local to the city of Edessa (today Urfa in southeastern Turkey), Syriac grew to become a major language throughout the eastern Roman Empire, in Persia, and along the Silk Road to China. It flourished especially as a language of Christians, among whom it remains a living language to this day. Syriac is now spoken not only in the Middle East, but also by diaspora communities in Europe, Scandinavia, North America, and Australia.

Ancient Syriac Christianity, like its present day counterpart, developed in the midst of a multilingual, multicultural context.[2] Semitic and Hellenic

---

Ephrem, *HVirg* = Ephrem, *Hymns on Virginity*. Syriac ed. Edmund Beck, *Des heiligen Ephraem des Syrers Hymnen De Virginitate*, CSCO 223-24/ Scr. Syr. 94-95 (Louvain 1962); English trans. Kathleen McVey, *Ephrem the Syrian: Hymns* (New York: Paulist Press, 1989), 259-468.

Jacob of Serug, Hom., Bedjan and Brock = *Homilies of Mar Jacob of Sarug/ Homiliae Selectae Mar Jacobi Sarugensis*, ed. Paul Bedjan, 2nd ed. Sebastian P. Brock (Piscataway, NJ: Gorgias Press, 2006), 6 vols.

NPNF = *Select Library of the Nicene and Post-Nicene Fathers*.

2   For the development of Syriac as a language, see Sebastian P. Brock, "Greek and Syriac in Late Antique Syr-

cultures dominated its regions, with profound and
long-lasting influence. In constant interaction with
the developing Greek and Latin churches, Syriac
Christians yet cultivated distinctive traditions of
their own. Although a minority language overshad-
owed by other, more powerful cultures, Syriac was
able to be influenced by those cultures and also to
contribute to them in return.

Between the fourth and seventh centuries – the
period scholars call late antiquity – Syriac literature gave notable attention to women of the Bible.
Drawing widely from both the Old and New Testaments, Syriac writers explored and imaginatively
expanded the stories of characters such as Eve "the
Mother of Life," Sarah the wife of Abraham, Tamar
the daughter-in-law of Judah, Potiphar's Wife, Jephthah's Daughter, Ruth the Moabite, Rahab the
prostitute of Jericho, the Widow of Sarepta who

ia," in *Literacy and Power in the Ancient World*, ed. Alan
K. Bowman and Greg Woolf (Cambridge: Cambridge
University Press, 1994), 149-60; and David G.K. Tay-
lor,"Bilingualism and Diglossia in Syria and Mesopota-
mia," in *Bilingualism in Ancient Society: Language Con-
tact and the Written Text*, ed. J.N. Adams, Mark Janse,
and Simon Swain (Oxford: Oxford University Press,
2002), 298-331. On the cultural complexity of the
larger region, see Kevin Butcher, *Roman Syria and the
Near East* (Los Angeles: J. Paul Getty Museum/Getty
Publications, 2003), especially 223-334; Fergus Millar,
The Roman Near East, 31 B.C. to A.D. 337 (Cambridge,
MA: Harvard University Press, 1993).

served the prophet Elijah, the Shunammite Woman who honored the prophet Elisha, Susanna the falsely accused matron, and the Mother of the Maccabean martyrs; the Virgin Mary, her kinswoman Elizabeth, the prophetess Anna, the Sinful Woman who wept at the feet of Christ, Mary Magdalene, Mary and Martha of Bethany, the Samaritan Woman, the Canaanite Woman, and more. Women of the Bible were presented across the whole array of Syriac literary genres as paradigmatic figures through whom to consider how the Christian life should be lived. Regardless of the literary form, these presentations offered – or assumed - imaginative narrative expansions of the biblical text, often with extensive speeches by the woman in monologue or in dialogue with another character (usually male) from the biblical account.

Syriac interest in women of the Bible may be seen even at the basic level of manuscript transmission. As early as the fifth and sixth centuries, Syriac manuscripts contained collections known as the "Book of Women," in which the books of Ruth, Esther, Judith, Susanna, and sometimes Thecla the companion of Paul were gathered together.[3] Attention was demon-

---

3   Catherine Burris and Lucas Van Rompay, "Thecla in Syriac Christianity: Preliminary Observations," *Hugoye* 5.2 (July 2002) [http://syrcom.cua.edu/Hugoye/Vol-5No2/HV5N2BurrisVanRompay.html]. Lucas Van Rompay, "'*No Evil Word About Her*': The Two Syriac Verions of the Book of Judith," in *Text, Translation, and*

strated further in the hugely popular extracanonical
stories and legends that circulated widely through
ancient Christian and Jewish communities, often in
Syriac versions, carrying extracanonical narratives
of biblical figures like Adam and Eve, Joseph and
Asenath, the mother of the Maccabean martyrs, or
the Virgin Mary.[4] Biblical women received marked
notice in Syriac biblical commentaries. Here Syriac
authors displayed learned command of Greek scholarship from the Christian schools of Alexandria and
Antioch as well as familiarity with Jewish intellec-

---

*Tradition: Studies on the Peshitta and its Use in the Syriac
Tradition Presented to Konrad D. Jenner on the Occasion
of his Sixty-Fifth Birthday*, ed. W.Th. Van Peursen and
R.B. ter Haar Romeny (Leiden: Brill, 2006), 205-30.

4   E.g., Gary Anderson, *The Genesis of Perfection: Adam
and Eve in Jewish and Christian Imagination* (Louisville:
Westminster John Knox Press, 2001); Ross Shepard
Kraemer, *When Aseneth Met Jospeh: A Late Antique
Tale of the Biblical Patriarch and His Egyptian Wife, Re-
considered* (New York: Oxford University Press, 1998);
Gerard Rouwhorst, "The Cult of the Seven Maccabean
Brothers and their Mother in Christian Tradition,"
in *Saints and Role Models in Judaism and Christianity*,
ed. Marcel Poorthuis and Joshua Schwartz (Leiden:
Brill, 2004), 183-204; Witold Witakowski, "Mart(y)
Shmuni, the Mother of the Maccabean Martyrs in Syr-
iac Tradition," in *VI Symposium Syriacum 1992*, ed. R.
Lavenant, Orientalia Christiana Analecta 247 (Rome
1994), 153-68; Stephen J. Shoemaker, *Ancient Tradi-
tions of the Virgin Mary's Dormition and Assumption*
(Oxford: Oxford University Press, 2002).

tual developments.[5] Above all, appreciation for biblical women was deeply incised into the late antique liturgical poetry, both hymns and verse homilies, for which Syriac is justly famous.[6] In all of these areas, Syriac authors show intimate connections to, and appreciation for, the narrative aggada of Jewish tradition, in an apparently quite different relation than Greek or Latin authors showed to the same material.[7]

---

5   Lucas Van Rompay, "The Christian Syriac Tradition of Interpretation," in *Hebrew Bible/Old Testament: The History of its Interpretation*, vol. 1: *From the Beginnings to the Middle Ages (Until 1300)*, part 1: *Antiquity*, ed. Magne Saebo (Göttingen: Vandenhoeck and Ruprecht, 1996), 612-41; idem, "Between the School and the Monk's Cell: The Syriac Old Testament Commentary Tradition," in *The Peshitta: Its Use in Literature and Liturgy: Papers Read at the Third Peshitta Symposium*, ed. R.B. ter Haar Romeny (Leiden: Brill, 2006), 27-51.

6   S.A. Harvey, "Spoken Words, Voiced Silence: Biblical Women in Syriac Tradition," *Journal of Early Christian Studies* 9 (2001): 105-31.

7   Adam Kamesar, "The Evaluation of the Narrative Aggada in Greek and Latin Patristic Literature," *Journal of Theological Studies* n.s.45 (1994): 37-71; Sebastian P. Brock, "Jewish Traditions in Syriac Sources," *Journal of Jewish Studies* 30 (1979): 212-32. But see also Galit Hasan-Rokem, "Narratives in Dialogue: a Folk Literary Perspective on Interreligious Contacts in the Holy Land in Rabbinic Literature of Late Antiquity," in *Sharing the Sacred: Religious Contacts and Conflicts in the Holy Land, First – Fifteenth Centuries CE*, ed. Arieh

Biblical women in Syriac tradition merit the attention of scholars for several reasons. First, Syriac writers granted these women a prominence often lacking in the biblical narratives themselves and not necessarily shared in the related traditions of Greek or Latin Christian or Jewish writers. The strikingly positive, powerful portrayal of these women in Syriac texts – often in contrast to far less flattering representations of the relevant male characters – is both literarily and theologically arresting. These portrayals sometimes challenged prevailing social norms even as they re-inscribed traditional cultural codes. Syriac authors across the spectrum of literary quality participated in this presentation of biblical women: from the brilliant work of Ephrem Syrus (d. 373) or Jacob of Serug (d. 521), to the poignant simplicity of the anonymous, village dialogue hymns (roughly 5th century through the medieval period).

Second, Syriac homilists and hymnographers favored literary forms that gave voice to the biblical characters. Where biblical stories generally portrayed women in the background with little if any spoken contribution, the Syriac poets would provide first-person speeches, sometimes as interior monologues but more often as external dialogues with other, usually male, biblical characters. The construction of the subjectivity of these biblical women in their first-

Kofsky & Guy G. Stroumsa (Jerusalem: Yad Izhak Ben Zvi 1998), 109-29.

person speech raises important questions about the function of gendered voices in religious and social identity formation and negotiation.

Third, and perhaps most hauntingly, in Syriac civic liturgies – that is, the worship activities of urban churches rather than monastic communities - women's choirs performed the hymns. Separate male and female choirs were active in Syriac civic churches both in the eastern Roman Empire and outside, in Persia, by the fourth century CE. They were comprised of consecrated men and women known as the Sons and Daughters of the Covenant, who worked in the service of local bishops.[8] The distinctive presence and participation of these choirs meant that Syriac liturgies offered biblical stories in diverse forms and by different participants: clergy, deacons, congregants, male and female choirs. Through rhetorical construction and ritual performance, gendered voices taught, expanded, and retold biblical stories to the larger Christian community as a means of doctrinal instruction.

A brief sketch of the broader historical context will help to situate these important issues of Syriac tradition.

---

8   S.A. Harvey, "Revisiting the Daughters of the Covenant: Women's Choirs and Sacred Song in Ancient Syriac Christianity," *Hugoye* 8.2 (July 2005) [http://syrcom.cua.edu/Hugoye/Vol8No2/HV8N2Harvey.html].

II. The Historical Context

Syriac attention to women of the Bible happened at a particular historical moment. Like their Greek and Latin counterparts both Christian and Jewish, late antique Syriac writers showed endless fascination with the Bible. They delighted in exploring the stories, filling in the gaps, and imagining what might have been thought or said or felt. Their interest was also a response to their circumstances.

Late antiquity was a time of rapid growth in Christian communities throughout the ancient Mediterranean world. The legalization of Christianity in the Roman Empire in 312 by the Emperor Constantine, and subsequent imperial favor for the new religion, brought a huge influx of converts. The situation was often turbulent, as church leaders worked to unify and stabilize ecclesiastical organization, structures, worship, and devotional practices. More fundamentally, they struggled for agreement on biblical canon and theological doctrine.[9] In this situation, they also struggled to educate their congregations. At a time when few people could or would have owned their own books, Christians needed to learn the Bible and its stories, just as they needed to learn orthodox doctrine ("right belief"). Since both matters were areas of ongoing contention, congregational instruction

---

9   Joseph Lynch, *Early Christianity: A Brief History* (New York: Oxford University Press, 2010) is an excellent overview to the entire period.

was a serious issue. Hymns and homilies were often designed for just this purpose: to teach (the right) biblical stories and the 'right way' to understand them. They were crucial tools in the task of educating a growing Christian population.[10] The liturgy became the church's school, a focus characteristic of late antiquity. Attention to biblical characters of all kinds, as well as to biblical women, was part of this larger ecclesiastical effort.

The choice of literary genres here is also important. Hymns and homilies were literary forms composed for public performance and participation. Their content was intended to educate, inspire, mold, and guide the larger Christian congregation.[11] Commentaries functioned differently, although the same writers were sometimes involved. By and large, commentaries were the preserve of the scholarly elite, a small (usually male) group with privileged access to

10   Mary B. Cunningham, "Preaching and the Community," in *Church and People in Byzantium: 20th Spring Symposium of Byzantine Studies, University of Manchester 1986*, ed. Rosemary Morris (Birmingham: Center for Byzantine Studies, 1986), 29-46; John A. McGuckin, "Poetry and Hymnography (2): The Greek World," *The Oxford Handbook of Early Christian Studies*, ed. S.A. Harvey and D.G. Hunter (Oxford: Oxford University Press, 2008), 641-56.

11   While we have some hymns in Greek and Latin that seem to have been composed for private pleasure or use, this kind of stratification does not characterize Syriac liturgical poetry.

texts and scholarship, including the work of scholars in other languages and other religious traditions.

If hymns and homilies contained biblical portraits that were livelier, bolder, or even shocking in comparison with scholarly commentaries, we should not be surprised. Preachers and choirs were competing not only with other churches and other religions, but also with other forms of public entertainment. Late antique cities cultivated a flourishing civic culture in which public entertainment, games, spectacles, mimes and pantomimes were integral to civic life.[12] In fact, late antique Roman Syria was famous for its theaters and the performances they offered.[13]

12   On the cultural significance of performance in late antique urban life, see now Ruth Webb, *Demons and Dance: Performance in Late Antiquity* (Cambridge, MA: Harvard University Press, 2008), and also Gregory S. Aldrete, *Gestures and Acclamations in Ancient Rome* (Baltimore: Johns Hopkins University Press, 1999); Blake Leyerle, *Theatrical Shows and Ascetic Lives: John Chrysostom's Attack on Spiritual Marriage* (Berkeley: University of California Press, 2001); Dennis Potter, "Entertainers in the Roman Empire," in *Life, Death and Entertainment in the Roman Empire*, ed. D.S. Potter and D.J. Mattingly (Ann Arbor: University of Michigan Press, 1999), 256-325; Fritz Graf, "Gestures and conventions: the gestures of Roman actors and orators," in *A Cultural History of Gesture*, ed. Jan Bremmer and Herman Roodenburg (Ithaca, NY: Cornell University Press, 1991), 36-58.

13   For the Syriac-speaking region in particular, see Butcher, *Roman Syria*, 223-69. Leyerle, *Theatrical*

Christian preachers regularly railed against theatrical shows, which they saw as insidious, dangerous to civic harmony, and detrimental to moral and ethical formation.[14] In such a climate, churches needed to offer instruction that was engaging and lively. At the same time, liturgy served the broader populace: rich and poor, male and female, young and old were present. Hymnographers and homilists needed to be inclusive in their teaching.[15] The strong accounts

---

Shows, 13-41, draws a vivid picture of late antique theater especially in Antioch. See Butcher, *Roman Syria*, 334-98 on the intersections of competing religions in the cultural sphere; Warwick Ball, *Rome in the East: The Transformation of an Empire* (New York: Routledge, 2000), 246-359, is also useful on urban layout and civic culture.

14   For a Syriac example, see e.g., Cyril Moss, "Jacob of Serugh's Homilies on the Spectacles of the Theatre," *Le Muséon* 48 (1935): 87-112; Leyerle, *Theatrical Shows*, 42-74.

15   Jaclyn Maxwell, *Christianization and Communication in Late Antiquity: John Chrysostom and his Congregation in Antioch* (Cambridge: Cambridge University Press, 2006); M. Cunningham, "Preaching and Community"; Mary B. Cunningham and Pauline Allen, *Preacher and Audience: Studies in Early Christian and Byzantine Homiletics* (Leiden: Brill 1998), esp. Wendy Mayer, "John Chrysostom: Extraordinary Preacher, Ordinary Audience," 105-38; Agnes Cunningham, "Women and Preaching in the Patristic Age," in David G. Hunter, ed., *Preaching in the Patristic Age. Studies in Honor of Walter J. Burghardt, S.J.* (Mahwah, NJ: Paulist, 1989), 53-72.

of biblical women we find in Syriac liturgical poetry
were surely there in part to minister to the women in
the congregations.

The literary characteristics of hymns and verse
homilies also distinguished them as genres of biblical instruction. Hymns and verse homilies were
forms of poetry. Rendered in meter, they were voiced
as heightened speech. Neither their sound nor their
syntax accorded with the ordinary language of nor-
mal conversation. Moreover, they were written to
be chanted, intoned, and sung in the sacred space
of worship. Whether in the domestic intimacy of
household piety, or at cemeteries or shrines, or in civic processions, or in formal church buildings where
the entire community of faithful came together, the
very form of hymns and verse homilies contributed
ritual authority to the occasion.[16]

In turn, the context of sacred ritual lent authority
to the words of liturgical poetry. The flow of ritual
order, the sequence of prayers, processions, readings,

16   A number of recent scholarly studies have analyzed
     the religious signification of hearing as a mode of experi-
     ence and epistemology. See especially David Chidester,
     Word and Light: Seeing, Hearing and Religious Discourse
     (Urbana, IL: University of Illinois Press, 1992); Leigh
     Eric Schmidt, *Hearing Things: Religion, Illusion, and the
     American Enlightenment* (Cambridge, MA: Harvard
     University Press, 2000), 1-37; David Howes, *The Va-
     rieties of Sensory Experience: A Sourcebook in the An-
     thropology of the Senses* (Toronto: University of Toronto
     Press, 1991).

hymns, homily (sometimes more than one), and the Eucharist itself, unfolded in a pattern of orchestrated interaction between the various participants.[17] The congregation was as central to the ritual whole as the members of the clergy or the choir.[18] They served as dialogic partners through the exchange of their sung responses and their choreographed patterns of standing, kneeling, prostrations, and other ritual gestures (the sign of the cross, the kiss of peace). Their reception of the heightened sensory environment was essential to the ritual process itself. They inhaled the rich scents of incense and holy oil; they gazed upon the abundant decor that adorned even village churches of late antiquity with fine linens, tapestries, frescoes, and mosaics. They rustled

---

17 This entire discussion is influenced by Catherine Bell, *Ritual Theory, Ritual Practice* (New York: Oxford University Press, 1992); see also Richard McCall, *Do This: Liturgy as Performance* (Notre Dame, IN: University of Notre Dame Press, 2007). On the importance of giving the women's choir due attention, in particular, see Teresa Berger, *Women's Ways of Worship: Gender Analysis and Liturgical History* (Collegeville, MN: Liturgical Press, 1999).

18 A good summary may be had in E. Braniste, "The Liturgical Assembly and its Functions in the *Apostolic Constitutions*," *Roles in the Liturgical Assembly: The Twenty-Third Liturgical Conference Saint Serge*, trans. M. O'Connell (New York: Pueblo Pub. Co., 1981), 73-100. The *Apostolic Constitutions* circulated widely in Syriac communities in late antiquity.

amidst the embroidered tapestries and vestments, filling their ears with lavish sounds of song, chant, and exhortation. They venerated holy ground, image, priest or bishop by ritual touch; they tasted the sweetness of wine and bread. These were not passive moments of observation, but active participation in the work of the liturgy.[19] That work was more than collective worship of the divine. It was also the collective process by which a community defined itself. Religious ritual designated its internal order by rank, gender, and class. It established and maintained connections between the participants, and to the larger social, economic, and political structures of which they were part. Private and domestic piety followed simplified patterns, but there, too, order, posture, gesture, incense and sequenced speech crafted a ritual efficacy tied to that of the church's formal liturgy. The chanting of Psalms was invariably part of such "smaller" practices, so that poetry provided a constant and defining characteristic of Christian piety, whether individual or collective.

In this densely textured ritual environment, liturgical poetry was not presented as in a concert to an audience. Rather, it was interwoven within a layered dialogue of verbal and gestural exchange.

19   On the importance of sense perception in the late antiquity liturgy, see S.A. Harvey, *Scenting Salvation: Ancient Christianity and the Olfactory Imagination* (Berkeley: University of California Press, 2006), especially pp. 57-90.

The context of sacred ritual enhanced the meaning and heightened the importance of every word performed. Hence it also increased the significance of women's stories and words when they were liturgically conveyed. How such poetry was presented, when in the ritual sequence, from which ritual location, and by whom, were matters that contributed to its reception and meaning.

III. The Syriac Forms

Ancient Syriac is famous for its rich tradition of liturgical poetry, articulated in hymns and verse homilies (poetic sermons). *Madrashe* (sing. *madrasha*) were hymns of varying meters that presented the fundamental teachings of the church, often by recalling or re-telling biblical stories. Sometimes these hymns included passages with the imagined speech of biblical characters. For example, hymns on the Nativity feast often contained verses representing the thoughts or words of the Virgin Mary as she marveled at the miraculous birth of her son. Sung by women's choirs, these verses seemed to represent Mary's voice in the midst of the church's festive gathering. Some *madrashe* were structured in verse couplets, others into stanzas. Both would be punctuated by a short, repeated refrain. The male chanter might sing the verses and the women's choir the refrain, or the choir may have sung the verses and led the congregation in the refrain. A variety of sung interaction was possible for the worship participants.[20]

A favorite form of the *madrasha* was the *soghitha*, the dialogue hymn, sung antiphonally by male and female choirs and generally including a refrain for the congregation. These hymns often presented a biblical story through an imagined dialogue between two characters, such as Sarah and Abraham, or the Virgin Mary and the Archangel Gabriel or Joseph, or the Sinful Woman and Satan. The verses alternated between the two characters, in a dialogue that presented a conflict or disagreement requiring resolution.[21] For example, the Archangel Gabriel argued to

20   S.A. Harvey, "On Mary's Voice: Gendered Words in Syriac Marian Tradition," in *The Cultural Turn in Late Ancient Studies: Gender, Asceticism, and Historiography*, ed. Dale Martin and Patricia Cox Miller (Durham: Duke University Press, 2005), 63-86.

21   Robert Murray, "Aramaic and Syriac Dispute Poems and their Connections," in *Studia Aramaica*, ed. M.J. Geller, J.C. Greenfield, and M.P. Weitzman, Journal of Semitic Studies Supplement 4 (1995), 157-87; Sebastian P. Brock, "Dramatic Dialogue Poems," in *Symposium Syriacum IV*, ed. H.J.W. Drijvers, R. Lavenant, C. Molenberg, and G.J. Reinink, Orientalia Christiana Analecta 229 (Rome, 1987), 135-47; idem, "Syriac Dispute Poems: The Various Types," in *Dispute Poems and Dialogues in the Ancient and Mediaeval Near East: Forms and Types of Literary Debates in Semitic and Related Literature*, ed. G.J. Reinink and H.L.J. Vanstiphout, Orientalia Lovaniensia Analecta 42 (Leuven: Peeters, 1991), 109-20; Kristi Upson-Saia, "Caught in a Compromising

convince the Virgin Mary that his promise of virgin birth was God-sent and genuine. Mary argued back her skepticism at this seeming impossibility and her determination not to be deceived by a divine visitor, as her foremother Eve had once been deceived in Eden by the serpent.[22] Or, in other hymns, Mary argued with Joseph over her claim to virginity despite her pregnancy.[23] In these hymns, again, women's choirs sang the imagined words of biblical women, lending immediacy and color to their performance in the collective worship of the gathered community.

The other major form of Syriac liturgical poetry was the verse homily, the *mimra* (pl. *mimre*). This was a prose-like presentation intoned in metered isosyllabic couplets, generally in patterns of 7 + 7 or 12 + 12. The verse homily was intoned or chanted by bishop, priest or deacon. Many ancient Syriac homilies retell biblical stories in imaginatively rich dramatic narratives.[24] Here, as in the hymns, bibli-

Position: The Biblical Exegesis and Characterization of Biblical Protagonists in the Syriac Dialogue Hymns," *Hugoye* 9.2 (July 2006) [http://syrcom.cua.edu/Hugoye/Vol9No2/HV9N2UpsonSaia.html].

22 Anon., "Mary and the Angel," trans. Brock, *Bride of Light*, 111-18.

23 Anon., "Mary and Joseph," trans. Brock, *Bride of Light*, 118-24.

24 Sebastian P. Brock, "Dramatic Narrative Poems on Biblical Topics in Syriac," *Studia Patristica* (forthcoming).

cal women sometimes take a central role, or gain importance far beyond what the biblical text itself contained. But in the homilies, their words were voiced by male presenters, with a different resonance than the women's choirs offered.[25]

By the fourth century, the Syriac eucharistic liturgy was a well-established service in a two-part structure similar to those celebrated in Latin and Greek.[26] The first part, the 'Liturgy of the Word,' revolved around the lectionary readings of the day and the homiletic expounding thereon. Verses of madrashe (doctrinal hymns) might be interspersed with Psalms in preface to the lectionary readings; the mimra (verse homily) would follow the Gospel. Thus both forms of poetry contributed to the instructional aspects of the service. The second part of the liturgy was the Eucharist itself: the offering of, consecration of, and partaking in the sacramental bread and wine. Only a few set hymns (such as the Sanctus) might be sung in this portion of the service, although there may have been

---

25   Harvey, "In Mary's Voice."

26   For the development of the Syriac liturgy and the daily offices in the context of eastern Christianity see, e.g., Juan Mateos, Lelya-Sapra: Essai d'interprétation des matines chaldéennes, Orientalia Christiana Analecta 156 (Rome: Pontificium Institutum Orientalium Studiorum, 1959); idem, La célébration de la parole dans la liturgie Byzantine, Orientalia Christiana Analecta 191 (Rome, Pontificium Institutum Orientalium Studiorum 1971).

hymns during the receiving of communion. Appropriately, most Syriac liturgical poetry was performed in the first part of the service, the Liturgy of the Word, as befitting the primarily didactic purpose of these hymns and verse homilies.

Often the madrashe (doctrinal hymns) for which Syriac is famous were sung at other types of services, especially the night vigil. The vigil was a highly flexible service in late antiquity, and local practices differed.[27] Varying in length and purpose, vigil services needed flexible components that could be added as needed. There were biblical readings from the lectionary, psalms, litanies, prayers, and hymns of different kinds. One or more homilies were chanted, not always newly preached; homilies by great preachers of the past, such as John Chrysostom or Jacob of Serug might be intoned, as well.[28] The reading of hagiography or martyrs' passions was also common.

---

27   Paul Bradshaw, *Daily Prayer in the Early Church* (Oxford: Oxford University Press, 1982), 72-110; Robert Taft, *The Liturgy of the Hours in East and West: The Origins of the Divine Office and its Meaning for Today* (Collegeville, MN: Liturgical Press, 1986), esp. 225-48.

28   Syriac Christianity demonstrated great reverence for John Chrysostom. His *Homilies on Matthew* were available in two different Syriac translations already by the mid-fifth century: Jeffrey W. Childers, "Patristic citations and versional evidence: The Syriac version[s] of Chrysostom's Homilies on Matthew and the Old Syriac text," *Le Muséon* 115 (2002): 129-56; idem, "Chrysostom's exegetical homilies on the New Testament in

In this context, hymns were both fitting to the nature of the service and also a good way to fill the time
constructively. Hymns provided a means for teaching and reflecting on the biblical or other readings, or
the purpose of the feast. They could include congregational participation (which helped to keep people
engaged), or different kinds of performance, as when
the female and male choirs sang the dialogue hymns
antiphonally. The dialogue hymns in particular may
have included elements of liturgical drama.[29] Hymns
provided variety in the service, an aspect important
especially for services that lasted through the night.
Ephrem alludes in several of his *Hymns on the Nativity* to the problems of sleepy or bored or distracted
worshippers.[30] Jacob of Serug worried about the
same problem even in Eucharistic liturgies.[31]

Syriac translation," *Studia Patristica* 33, ed. E.A. Liv-
ingstone (Leuven: Peeters, 1997), 509-16. More generally, Chrysostom was a fundamental source in Syriac
biblical commentaries. See Lucas Van Rompay, "Past
and Present Perceptions of Syriac Literary Tradition,"
Hugoye 3.1 (2000) [http://syrcom.cua.edu/Hugoye/
Vol3No1/HV3N1VanRompay.html].

29   See Sebastian P. Brock, "The Dispute Between the
Cherub and the Thief," *Hugoye* 5.2 (2002) [http://
syrcom.cua.edu/Hugoye/Vol5No2/HV5N2Brock.
html].

30   E.g., Ephrem, *HNat* 1: 72, 77-81; 4: 51-52; 5: 6-7,
9; 21: 2, 10.

31   Jacob of Serug, "On Ephrem," vv.128, 145-47, 169,
trans. Joseph P. Amar, "A Metrical Homily on Holy

Syriac tradition was also notable for the diverse ways this poetry was performed in worship services or other public devotional gatherings. In fact, poetic performance highlighted the attention to biblical women in Syriac liturgies.[32] Perhaps uniquely in ancient Christianity, Syriac churches developed a tradition of including women's choirs in the liturgy.[33] Their task was to sing the madrashe (doctrinal hymns), including the soghyatha (dialogue hymns). The choirs are attested in the hymns of Ephrem during the fourth century, and by the sixth century their establishment was attributed to him.[34] In church canons for both the eastern and western Syriac churches, in both the Persian and Roman Empires, fifth and sixth century church canons mandate the presence of these choirs in every village, town, and city church, as well as designating their responsibility for the madrashe (doctrinal hymns), sung at

Mar Ephrem by Mar Jacob of Sarug," *Patrologia Orientalis* 47 (Turnhout: Brepols, 1995): 1-76, at 57, 63, 67; Jacob of Serug, Hom. 95, "Homily On the Partaking of the Holy Mysteries," trans. Amir Harrak (Piscataway, NJ: Gorgias Press, 2009), vv. 123-26, p. 18.

32 Harvey, "Spoken Words, Voiced Silence."

33 I have collected much of the evidence from the third century through the tenth in Harvey, "Revisiting the Daughters of the Covenant."

34 Jacob of Serug, "On Ephrem;" Joseph P. Amar, *The Syriac 'Vita' Tradition of Ephrem the Syrian* (Ann Arbor, 1988).

morning and evening services as well as feasts, saints' days, and funerals (although not at the cemetery).[35] Their presence is evident also in literary sources that attest to their public prominence,[36] as well as to their fundamental role in the liturgical life of local communities.[37]

The role of Syriac women's choirs raises major issues for our understanding of women in ancient Christianity more broadly. The presence of these choirs is a distinctive feature of the Syriac-speaking churches, in comparison with Greek and Latin churches to their west. These certainly cultivated

---

35   Canons 20, 27, in "The Rules of Rabbula for the Clergy and the Qeiama," ed. and trans. Arthur Vööbus, *Syriac and Arabic Documents Regarding Legislation Relative to Syrian Asceticism*, Papers of the Estonian School of Theology in Exile 11 (Stockholm, 1960), at pp. 34-50; Amar, *Syriac Vita*, p. 296, 298 (Syriac on pp. 157, 158-59); "Maruta Canons," 26.1-3, 41.1, 26.4, 41.3, ed. and trans. in Arthur Vööbus, *The Canons Ascribed to Maruta of Maipherqat and Related Sources*, CSCO 439-40/ Scr. Syr. 191-92 (Louvain 1982); J.B. Chabot, *Synodicon Orientale ou Recueil de Synodes Nestoriens* (Paris: Imprimerie Nationale, 1902), on pp. 221-22 (Syr.), p. 486 (Fr.).

36   *The Chronicle of Pseudo-Joshua the Stylite*, trans. Frank R. Trombley and John W. Watt (Liverpool: Liverpool University Press, 2000), at ch. 36, pp. 34-36. See also chs. 43, 100.

37   John of Ephesus, *Lives of the Eastern Saints*, 16; ed. and trans. E.W. Brooks, *Patrologia Orientalis* 17 (Paris 1923), on pp. 229-47.

congregational singing as well as choirs of nuns, for whom the chanting of Psalms was an important part of their daily discipline, as described by Basil of Caesarea.[38] Female monastic choirs also sang on the major feasts, as famously recorded by the western pilgrim Egeria for the Easter liturgy in Jerusalem.[39] Important public funerals might also have choirs of nuns performing, such as described by Gregory of Nyssa for his sister Macrina late in the fourth century, or for the great fifth century bishop Rabbula of Edessa (d. 436) at whose funeral there were said to have been eighteen choirs of deaconesses.[40]

But there was also a persistent opposition to women's liturgical singing that recurs in Greek and Latin literature, and which has influenced modern schol-

---

38   Basil, Ep 2.12, 207.3. These and other primary sources are conveniently collected in James McKinnon, *Music in Early Christian Literature* (Cambridge: Cambridge University Press, 1987), here at 68-69.

39   Egeria, *Diary of a Pilgrimage*, 24; trans. George E. Gingras, Ancient Christian Writers 38 (New York: Paulist Press, 1970), on pp. 89-93.

40   Gregory of Nyssa, *Life of Macrina*, trans. Virginia Callahan, *Saint Gregory of Nyssa: Ascetical Works*, Fathers of the Church 58 (Washington, DC, 1967), 171, 178, 182-83, 186-87; *The Heroic Deeds of Mar Rabbula*, trans. Robert Doran, *Stewards of the Poor: The Man of God, Rabbula, and Hiba in Fifth-Century Edessa* (Kalamazoo, MI: Cistercian Publications, 2006), 65-105, at p. 104.

arship on the subject.[41] Christian leaders as diverse
as Cyril of Jerusalem in the mid-fourth century or
Isidore of Pelusium (Egypt) at the turn of the fifth
century periodically admonished that women should
be quiet and not even join in the congregational
hymns, citing the New Testament passages that ex-
hort women to keep silence (I Cor 14:33-5; I Tim
2:11-12).[42] The chronically caustic Latin scholar Jerome firmly agreed.[43] Although instances of women's
monastic choirs in public liturgy do appear in late
antique Greek literature, we can sense the tension
in a variant of the Mary of Egypt story contained
in Cyril of Skythopolis's *Life of Cyriacus* (sixth century). In this version, the hermit Mary describes her
previously sinful life in this way: "I became a cantor

---

41   The most extensive treatment remains the problem-
     atically outdated work of Johannes Quasten, *Music and
     Worship in Pagan and Christian Antiquity*, trans. Boni-
     face Ramsey (Washington, DC: National Association
     of Pastoral Musicians, 1983). In the original 1973 pub-
     lication of this book in German, Quasten essentially
     presented the work of his doctoral thesis from 1927.
     See also idem, "The Liturgical Singing of Women in
     Christian Antiquity," *Catholic Historical Review* 27
     (1941): 149-65.

42   Cyril Jer., *Procat.* 14; Isidore, *Ep.* 1, 90; McKinnon,
     Music in Early Christian Literature, pp. 75 and 61, re-
     spectively.

43   Jerome, *Dialog contra pel.*, 1, 25; McKinnon, p. 145.

of the holy church of the Resurrection of Christ, and the devil made many scandalized with me."[44]

In contrast, Syriac writers mention women's choirs as intrinsic to the beauty of liturgy, even as their singing contributed to what the liturgy taught: "the recesses of our ears are filled with the musical strains of virgins."[45] Jacob of Serug (d. 521) urged people to attend to the teaching role of these choirs: "Pay heed to the hymns (sung) by the virgins with glorious voices/ that the wisdom of the Most High has given to the congregations."[46] Jacob is one of the most important sources on these choirs. He discussed them at length in his panegyrical homily on St. Ephrem, where he claimed that Ephrem had founded women's choirs to sing the doctrinal hymns he composed. Their work, sang Jacob, was at once glorious and ar-

---

44 Cyril of Scythopolis, *Life of Cyriacus*, sec. 18; trans. R.M. Price, *Cyril of Scythopolis, Lives of the Monks of Palestine* (Kalamazoo, MI: Cistercian Publications, 1991), at p. 257. I am indebted to Daniel Caner for this reference.

45 Ephrem, *Hymns on Easter* 2: 8; trans. Sidney Griffith in McKinnon, *Music*, pp. 93-94. The entire passage is a vivid depiction of the whole church gathered in worship, with each person or group identified with a different task. Compare Jacob of Serug, *Adv. Iud.* 7: 529-42, ed. and trans. Micheline Albert, "Jacques de Saroug, Homélies contre les Juifs," *Patrologia Orientalis* 38 (1976): 216-17.

46 Jacob of Serug, "On the Partaking of the Holy Mysteries," vv. 131-32, trans. Harrak at p. 18.

resting, teaching as much by their sheer presence as
by the words they sang:

> Behold, the gatherings of the glorious (church)
> resound with their melodies.
> A new sight of women uttering the proclamation;
> And behold, they are called teachers among the
> congregations.[47]

Women's choirs continue in Syriac churches even
now. Documentation after the medieval period is
hard to find, but since the late twentieth century an
energetic revival of these choirs has been underway
in the Middle East and Europe.[48]

In late antiquity, the Syriac women's choirs became
important at the very moment that Christianity in
the Roman Empire was decreasing the leadership
of women and marginalizing women's authoritative
or public religious roles. This was the period when
female deacons and consecrated widows gradually
disappeared throughout the churches of the Roman

---

47 Jacob of Serug, "On Ephrem," vv. 41-42; trans. Amar,
    at p. 35.

48 S.A. Harvey, "Performance as Exegesis: Women's
    Liturgical Choirs in Syriac Tradition," in *Inquiries into
    Eastern Christian Worship: Acts of the Second Interna-
    tional Congress of the Society of Oriental Liturgy*, ed.
    Basilius J. Groen and Steven Hawkes Teeples, Eastern
    Christian Studies 10 (Leuven: Peeters, forthcoming).

Empire.[49] Even more surprising is the issue of what
these choirs sang.[50] Syriac commentators and church
canons alike state that the women's choirs must sing
the madrashe, the doctrinal hymns through which
the larger church was instructed in right belief, prop-
er biblical understanding, and faithful living.[51] These
hymns, explicitly doctrinal, addressed the same top-

---

49   For women's offices in the early church, see Ute E.
      Eisen, *Women Officeholders in Early Christianity: Epi-
      graphical and Literary Studies*, trans. Linda M. Malo-
      ney (Collegeville, MN, 2000), and Kevin Madigan and
      Carolyn Osiek, *Ordained Women in the Early Church:
      A Documentary History* (Baltimore, MD, 2005). For
      the Syriac situation, see Sebastian P. Brock, "Deacon-
      esses in the Syriac Tradition," in *Women in Prism and
      Focus: Her Profile in Major World Religions and in Chris-
      tian Traditions*, ed. Prasanna Vazheeparampil (Rome:
      Mar Thoma Yogam/St. Thomas Christian Fellowship,
      1996), 204-17; S.A. Harvey, "Women's Service in An-
      cient Syriac Christianity," in *Mother, Nun, Deaconess:
      Images of Women According to Eastern Canon Law*, ed.
      Eva Synek, *Kanon* 16 (Egling 2000), 226-41.

50   See S.A. Harvey, "Revisiting the Daughters of the
      Covenant."

51   A useful collection of Greek and Latin primary
      sources on early Christian teaching may be found in
      Robert Eno, *Teaching Authority in the Early Church*,
      Message of the Fathers of the Church 14 (Wilmington,
      DE: Michael Glazier/Liturgical Press, 1984). How-
      ever, the teaching authority of the liturgical choir seems
      not to have been considered by most historians of early
      Christianity.

ics that were elsewhere in the great canonical manuals of the time expressly forbidden for women to teach: the birth, life, teachings, miracles, death and resurrection of Christ.[52] Syriac women's choirs were not uncontroversial.[53] Rather, their practice raised questions of gender, authority, social control, and the public, communal negotiation of these areas.

Scholars have given much attention to the capacity of holy women in late antiquity to attain high levels of spiritual authority among the general populace and to serve as spiritual teachers and counselors.[54] Yet their authority rested on a pattern of direct, even

52   E.g., *Didascalia Apostolorum*, ch. 15; ed. and trans. A. Vööbus, *The Didascalia Apostolorum in Syriac*, vol. 1, CSCO 401-2/Scr. Syr. 175-76, and vol. 2, CSCO 407-8/ Scr. Syr. 179-80 (Louvain, 1979), here at CSCO 408/Scr. Syr. 180, at pp. 144-45.

53   Emphasized especially in Kathleen McVey, "Ephrem the Kitharode and Proponent of Women: Jacob of Serug's Portrait of a Fourth-Century Churchman for the Sixth Century Viewer and its significance for the twenty-first century ecumenist," in *Orthodox and Wesleyan Ecclesiology*, ed. S.T. Kimbrough (Crestwood, NY, 2007), 229-53.

54   E.g., Elizabeth A. Clark, *Ascetic Piety and Women's Faith: Essays on Late Ancient Christianity* (Lewiston, NY: Edwin Mellen Press, 1986); Gillian Cloke, *This Female Man of God: Women and Spiritual Power in the Patristic Age 350-450* (New York: Routledge, 1995); Gillian Clark, *Women in Late Antiquity: Pagan and Christian Lifestyles* (New York: Oxford University Press, 1993).

personal instruction by a mentor to a devotee. The teaching performed by the Syriac women's choirs differed substantially from this model, both in kind and in nature. Their teaching communicated the collectively identified corporate doctrines of the Church, not the holy wisdom of a charismatic individual.

In the Syriac liturgy, then, Christians heard the imagined stories and voices of biblical women, sometimes voiced by women's choirs, sometimes by male chanters, priests, deacons, or bishops. Gendered performance contributed to the interpretations of the biblical texts being offered in song and sermon.[55] By special words (poetry) and in the special space of holy ritual (the liturgy wherever enacted), women's stories were rendered not only important, but also sacred. Ritual enhanced the significance of these stories. Performance became a mode of exegesis. What meaning did such presentations add to the stories of these women?

IV. TEACHING BIBLE WITH WOMEN'S VOICE

Biblical women appeared in Syriac hymns and homilies in clusters of similar types, or in focused individual close-ups, either of which could extend the woman's story far beyond the contours of the biblical text at hand. But Syriac writers did not have free rein to invent whatever they wished at random, in devel-

55   Harvey, "Performance as Exegesis."

oping these figures and their stories (unlike modern novelists or film-makers!). A number of factors guided their work.[56] For example, different biblical translations might suggest different characterizations of biblical figures: in this instance, the Syriac versions in comparison with the available Greek or Hebrew texts.[57]

So, for example, when Jacob of Serug composed his elegant homily on Jephthah's Daughter from Judges 11, his account of this young virgin sacrificed by her own father plays often with the Syriac term *ihidaytha*, "only-begotten," the term used for her in the Peshitta version (Jud 11:34). The same term is used in the Syriac Bible for Isaac, the *ihidaya*, "only-begotten" son of Abraham in Genesis 22:2, the account of the (near) sacrifice of Isaac; and for Jesus himself in John 3:16. The term allows Jacob's homily to interweave strong associations from Genesis 22 and the passion narratives with his presentation of the Daughter's story, lending majesty and profound

---

56   For an excellent discussion of the process by which a biblical figure would be constructed by late antique authors, see Kraemer, *When Aseneth Met Joseph*, 19-49.

57   Sebastian P. Brock, *The Bible in Syriac Tradition* (Piscataway, NJ: Gorgias Press, 2006). Even within these versions there could be variations: e.g., Van Rompay, "'*No Evil Word About Her*.'"

theological pathos to a tale which, in Judges 11, reads rather differently.[58]

Sometimes extracanonical narratives were familiar and influential to the point where they appeared to be part of the canon: the *Protevangelium of James*, for instance, with its account of the Virgin Mary's birth of Christ in a cave – a detail to which Ephrem Syrus refers in his *Hymns on the Nativity* without comment or gloss.[59] Biblical stories, like ancient mythologies, were constantly malleable, constantly re-told, with variations and additions that sometimes became part of public culture.[60]

Syriac writers presented biblical characters with avid imagination, but their portraits were also highly

---

58   Jacob of Serug, Hom. 159, "On Jephthah's Daughter," Bedjan and Brock, vol. 5, 306-30, trans. S.A. Harvey and Ophir Münz-Manor (Piscataway, NJ: Gorgias Press, 2010); and for a more detailed discussion, S.A. Harvey, "Bride of Blood, Bride of Light: Biblical Women as Images of Church in Jacob of Serug," *Malphono w-Rabo d-Malphone: Festschrift for Sebastian P. Brock*, ed. George Kiraz (Piscataway, NJ: Gorgias Press, 2008), 189-218.

59   Ephrem, *HNat* 13:10.

60   The ubiquitous scenes in eastern Christian art of the Nativity in a cave are one example of this. The numerous versions of the Aqedah in Gen 22, whether literary or visual, would be another: e.g., Edward Noort and Eibert Tigchelaar, eds., *The Sacrifice of Isaac: The Aqedah (Genesis 22) and its Interpretations* (Leiden: Brill, 2002).

stylized. The construction of characters from sometimes only a brief biblical mention followed patterns familiar from classical motifs, instilled through
school exercises in rhetoric, declamation, and ora-
tory.[61] They conformed to stock characters familiar
across the ancient Mediterranean world from literature, folklore, and theater:[62] the innocent virgin unjustly maligned, the pious widow, the seductive sinner, the righteous wife, the penitent harlot, the wise
prophet, the vulnerable child. For some, they drew
on tragic elements of fear, dread, horror, recognition
and catharsis. For others, they engaged comic tropes
of cunning, inversion, playfulness, misrecognition,
and humorous deception.

Through their portraits Syriac writers used biblical characters to personify virtues or vices, abstrac-
tions, roles, or positions. Like the figures of myth
explored through the pedagogical exercises of rheto-

61   On the classical basis of late antique Syriac educa-
     tion, even without Greek, see now Adam Becker, *The
     Fear of God and the Beginning of Wisdom: The School of
     Nisibis and Christian Scholastic Culture* (Philadelphia:
     University of Pennsylvania Press, 2006); also Jan Wil-
     lem Drijvers and Alasdair A. MacDonald, *Centres of
     Learning: Learning and Location in Pre-Modern Europe
     and the Near East* (Leiden: Brill, 1995).

62   Compare Kraemer, *When Aseneth Met Joseph*, 19-
     49; Michael L. Satlow, "Fictional Women: A Study in
     Stereotypes," in *The Talmud Yerushalmi and Graeco-
     Roman Culture*, ed. Peter Schäfer (Tübingen: Mohr
     Siebeck, 2003), 225-43.

ric and declamation, biblical characters served the work of moral formation and guidance for the larger Christian community.[63] Plotlines as well as character types followed similar patterns that appeared in Greek and Roman novels, the Christian apocryphal acts, and Jewish and Christian extracanonical narratives, in addition to the mimes and pantomimes performed in late antique theaters (which themselves re-told the familiar sagas of classical comedy and tragedy).

The stock types of the ancient literary imagination included powerful female characters. Yet recent scholarship has stressed that these imagined women should not be mistaken for social perceptions of real women, nor were they necessarily even directed towards an audience of women. Rather, they provided vehicles through which to negotiate the issues of religious, social, and cultural change at hand in late antiquity. And they did so with a view to resolving moral tensions or social dissonance among the male

---

63   Ruth Webb, "Poetry and Rhetoric," in *Handbook of Classical Rhetoric in the Hellenistic Period, 330 BC – AD 400*, ed. Stanley Porter (New York: Brill, 1997), 339-70; Richard Hawley, "Female Characterization in Greek Declamation," in *Ethics and Rhetoric: Classical Essays for Donald Russell on his Seventy-Fifth Birthday*, ed. Doreen Innes, Harry Hine, and Christopher Pelling (Oxford: Clarendon Press, 1995), 255-68; Robert A. Kaster, *Emotion, Restraint, and Community in Ancient Rome* (New York: Oxford University Press, 2005).

elites of society. The "work" of these literary and leg-
endary heroines serviced normative interests with
respect to the male-dominated structures of power
and authority.[64] We must keep this larger cultural
scenario in mind when considering the distinctive-
ness of Syriac biblical women. The authors of Syriac
liturgical poetry were men (although, to be fair, a
huge quantity of Syriac liturgical poetry is anonymous; it is at least possible that the women's choirs
or their deaconess directors may have done some of
the composing).[65] Some, like Ephrem, were notably
sympathetic to women and others not (e.g., Narsai).
The biblical women of Syriac imagination were ex-

---

64   Crucial work here will be found in Katharine
     Haynes, *Fashioning the Feminine in the Greek Novel*
     (New York: Routledge, 2003); Kate Cooper, *The Virgin
     and the Bride: Idealised Womanhood in Late Antiquity*
     (Cambridge, MA: Harvard University Press, 1996);
     Kraemer, *When Aseneth Met Joseph*, 191-221.

65   Technically speaking, no known text authored by a
     woman survives in Syriac from the ancient or medi-
     eval periods. The sixth century *Life of Febronia* claims
     to have been written by a nun, Thomais, who narrates
     the story; however, the narrator's role is also part of the
     artifice. More intriguing is the possibility of an anony-
     mous verse homily on Sarah and the sacrifice of Isaac,
     for the text contains an apparent self-reference by the
     author at the beginning, in what appears to be the first
     person feminine singular. See Sebastian P. Brock, "Two
     Syriac Verse Homilies on the Binding of Isaac," *Le Mu-
     séon* 99 (1986): 61-130, at pp. 98-99.

actly that: imagined, and invariably with a view to the moral edification of the civic community.[66] Female characters served the needs of the church congregation as a whole. We will return to this point in due course.

Late antiquity was a time of fierce religious competition. Christianity competed with other religions, and different Christian groups competed with one another. Telling biblical stories was also a polemical act. It claimed particular stories for one's own community, provided their correct interpretation, and championed a particular tradition of heroes and heroines. In what follows, I turn to some specific biblical women, to see how these issues played out in Syriac liturgical poetry.

I. EPHREM'S MARY AND
WOMEN OF SCANDAL

The anonymous sixth century *Life of St. Ephrem* claimed that Ephrem founded the women's choirs in order to counteract the seductive hymns sung by

---

66   On Ephrem's sympathetic portrayals of women, see Sebastian P. Brock, *The Luminous Eye: The Spiritual World Vision of Saint Ephrem the Syrian* (Kalamazoo, MI: Cistercian Publications, 1992), 168-72. For Narsai, see C. Molenberg, "Narsai's memra on the reproof of Eve's daughters and the <<tricks and devices>> they perform," *Le Muséon* 106 (1993): 65-87.

heretics in Edessa.[67] That is, the *vita* states that the
women's choirs were founded for polemical purposes. In Ephrem's *Hymns on Nativity* we can see the
situation in play.[68] The *Hymns on Nativity* are a collection of hymns Ephrem wrote for the feast over a
number of years.[69] These hymns celebrate the feast
with a great wealth of theological exploration, taking
up various themes and images in turn. As a group,
the hymns offer profound exaltation of the Virgin
Mary, unusually developed for such an early date
(mid-fourth century). A number of them also treat
other women of the Bible; and, in several instances,

67   *Syriac Vita*, ch. 30-31, Amar, p. 293-99, Syriac on pp.
      154-60.

68   Ephrem engaged in heated polemics with Bardaisan-
      ites, Manicheans, Marcionites, Valentinians, and Ari-
      ans in his hymns and prose refutations. His attacks on
      Jews permeate many of his writings. See now Christine
      Shepardson, *Anti-Judaism and Christian Orthodoxy:
      Ephrem's Hymns in Fourth Century Syria* (Washington,
      DC: The Catholic University of America Press, 2008);
      Sidney H. Griffith, "Setting Right the Church of Syria:
      Saint Ephrem's *Hymns against Heresies*," in *The Limits
      of Ancient Christianity: Essays on Late Antique Thought
      and Culture in Honor of R.A. Markus*, ed. W.E. Kling-
      shirn and M. Vessey (Ann Arbor, MI: University of
      Michigan, 1999), 97-114.

69   Ephrem did not compose them as a cycle, although
      he did collect the core group of sixteen hymns, to which
      later editors added others by Ephrem on the same
      theme to arrive at the present collection of twenty-eight
      hymns. McVey, *Ephrem*, 29.

Ephrem refers to the women's choir. Even a short consideration will show the critical role played by these women, biblical and historical, in the context in which Ephrem served.

Ephrem himself referred to his hymns on the Nativity as "lullabyes."[70] A number of them are sung in the first person, as Mary sings to her newborn son in prolonged meditation on her miraculous pregnancy and birth-giving. But who was this Mary, the subject of Ephrem's hymns, whose voice he represented through his choirs? Most often she takes the role of prophetess, echoing the voice of Mary from Luke's Magnificat, marveling at God's mighty works that have 'overthrown the orders' of men. In this mode, he portrays her wonder that God had chosen her, poor and unwed, betrothed to a struggling carpenter, from an undistinguished town, giving birth in the bare dirt of a cave. Addressing her son, she sings:

> … Because of You, a daughter of the poor
> is envied. Because of You, a daughter of the weak
> is an object of jealousy. Who gave you to me?
> Son of the Rich one, Who despised the womb
> Of rich women, what drew You
> Toward the poor? For Joseph is needy,
> And I am impoverished.[71]

---

70 McVey, *Ephrem*, 29.

71 *HNat* 15: 2-3.

How had things been brought to such a course? One of the (many) themes Ephrem presents in these hymns was the wonder of God's plan for human history. In Hymn 1 with sheeting cascades of lyrical poetry, he pours forth the names of Christ's ancestry from the genealogies in the gospels of Luke and Matthew.[72] With dizzying magnitude, he surveys the whole arc of time from Adam until the birth of Christ. Combining the two differing lists of Luke 3:23-38 and Matthew 1:1-16, Ephrem recasts the sagas of the Hebrew Bible to present biblical history as the steady, certain unfolding of God's plan for humankind, culminating in the birth of Christ and the establishment of the church. He thereby presents biblical history as *Christian* history. Luke's list of ancestors allowed Ephrem to reflect on human history from its origins with Adam and the first generations that followed up until the present. But Ephrem's wonder and praise in this hymn and others linger upon the lineage named by Matthew.

Early Christian commentators were well aware of the differences between the genealogies of Matthew and Luke. They feared the conflicting accounts made an easy target for critics, and were dismayed by the seeming contradictions between the two. Most embarrassing, however, was that Matthew's genealogy named five women, the Virgin Mary being the last. All the others were women of indisputably

---

72   *HNat* 1, trans. McVey 63-74.

ill-repute: Tamar the young widow who seduced her father-in-law Judah (Gen 38), Rahab the prostitute of Jericho (Josh 2:1-21, 6:17-25), Ruth the Moabite who climbed into the bed of Boaz (Ruth 3-4), and Bathsheba who committed adultery with King David while her husband was away at war (2 Sam 11-12). Why should Mary be placed among such company? Greek and Latin patristic authors rarely comment on this genealogy, almost invariably beginning their commentaries on Matthew at 1:17, to avoid the issue![73]

For its part, Matthew's genealogy had already indicated heated contest among first century Jews over who could claim the messianic lineage.[74] The women

---

73   See the discussion in S.A. Harvey, "Holy Impudence, Sacred Desire: The Women of Matthew 1:16 in Syriac Tradition," in *"If These Stones Could Speak …": Essays in Honor of Dennis Edward Groh*, ed. George Kalantzis and Thomas F. Martin (Lewiston, NY: Edwin Mellen Press, 2009), 29-50.

74   There is extensive scholarly discussion of the genealogies in Matthew and Luke and the issue of Matthew's women. See, e.g., Larry K. Lyke, "What Does Ruth Have to Do with Rahab? Midrash Ruth Rabbah and the Matthean Genealogy of Jesus," in Craig Evans and James Sanders, eds., *The Function of Scripture in Early Jewish and Christian Tradition* (Sheffield: Sheffield Academic Press, 1998), 262-84; Jane Schaberg, *The Illegitimacy of Jesus: A Feminist Theological Interpretation of the Infancy Narratives* (Sheffield: Sheffield Academic Press, 1995); J. P. Heil, "The Narrative Roles of the Women in

Matthew named had been included in earlier genealogies (Ruth 4:1-22, I Chron 2:1-15), where they
represented not only sexual misconduct but also
ethnic outsiders joining God's chosen people. In
Jewish commentators, these scandalous women were
"rehabilitated," their stories modified to be more fitting for their venerable role as foremothers of the
Messiah to come. Ephrem himself seemed to follow
suit for Tamar in his commentary on Genesis, sec.
34.1-6. However, in Ephrem's *Hymns on the Nativity*
the women of Matthew's genealogy are often men-
tioned, in terms that highlighted - and even glorified
- their scandalous behavior.[75]

In several of the *Hymns on the Nativity*, Ephrem re-
turns to the figures of Tamar, Rahab, and Ruth, and
then to Mary, emphasizing that these women all suffered slander and calumny because of their unshake-
able faith. All, he sings, were driven by a desire for
God's incarnation so powerful that it caused them
to act against propriety and social order. Knowing

Matthew's Genealogy," *Biblica* 72 (1991): 538-45; E.D.
Freed, "The Women in Matthew's Genealogy," *Journal
of New Testament Studies* 29 (1987): 3-19.

75   Crucial here are the studies of T. Kronholm, "Holy
Adultery: The Interpretation of the Story of Judah and
Tamar (Gen. 38) in the Genuine Hymns of Ephrem
Syrus," *Orientalia Suecana* 40 (1991): 149-63; P.J. Bo-
tha, "Ephrem the Syrian's treatment of Tamar in comparison to that in Jewish sources," *Acta Patristica et Byz-
antina* 6 (1995): 15-26.

God's promise of a messiah born of a chosen people, Tamar, Rahab, and Ruth pursued that promise with single-minded zeal. Driven by a sacred thirst, a hunger of devotion, a holy impudence, they had "stolen" and "seized" the blessed seed "hidden in the loins" of the house of Judah. Ephrem praises the fervency of their faith, despite its incitement of unseemly behavior. "By You [O Christ] honorable women made themselves contemptible … [holding] in contempt all other voices for the sake of Your voice."[76] Rather than diminishing the scandal of their efforts, he seems to exalt it. With imagery of stealth, deception, nets, and hunting, he extols the extremities to which their faith compelled them. "Tamar went out and in darkness/ she stole the light, and by filth/ she stole chastity, and by nakedness she entered furtively to You, the Honorable One."[77] But in Ephrem's song, Tamar's actions displayed no immorality. Instead, they showed her perfection:

> For the adultery of Tamar was chaste because of You …
> She desired You, pursued You, and even became a harlot for Your sake.
> For You she longed, You she kept [in memory], and she became a chaste woman. She loved You.[78]

---

76 Ephrem, *HNat* 9: 13-14; McVey, 127.

77 Ephrem, *HNat* 9: 8; McVey, 126.

78 Ephrem, *HNat* 9: 10-11; McVey, 126.

For these women, Ephrem sings, the birth of Christ justified their decisions and rewarded their offense. The Nativity vindicated these women, who chose their course with God's purpose as their only concern. God's choice to work salvation through the off-spring of these women was a shocking act. But then, God's choice of a virgin was itself a surprising, even disturbing reordering of society. Ephrem describes how the promise of a messiah's birth might have sparked other expectations:

> Women heard that behold a virgin indeed
> Would conceive and bring forth. Well-born women hoped
> That He would shine forth from them, and elegant women
> That He would appear from them. Blessed is Your height [O Lord]
> That bent down and shone forth from the poor.[79]

Like the scandalous foremothers, Mary's role was unlikely and unwelcome. Like the earlier women, Ephrem explained in song, she suffered persecution and slander for her pregnancy. In Ephrem's hymns Mary sings with confident yet troubled words: "with Your pure conception/ evil men have slandered me … For Your sake, behold, I am persecuted/ because I conceived and bore the One Place of Refuge/ for hu-

---

79   *HNat* 8: 20; McVey, 123.

man beings."[80] The memory of holy scandal gives her strength and comfort both, as Ephrem grants Mary her own voice:

> Behold, I am slandered and oppressed,
> But I rejoice. My ears are full
> Of scorn and disdain, but it is a small matter to me
> …
> Since I am not despised by You, my Son,
> I am confident. I who am slandered
> Have conceived and given birth to the True Judge
> Who will vindicate me. For if Tamar was acquitted by Judah, how much more will I be acquitted by You![81]

A number of the hymns imagine the scorn and ridicule to which Mary must have been subjected as her pregnancy took its course.[82] Ephrem marvels at the wondrous mysteries of divine action in choosing such a route: a holy conception that left Mary, in the eyes of the unknowing, indistinguishable from harlots.[83] Christians had long addressed such slander from their critics, both Pagan and Jewish. In

---

80 *HNat* 6: 3-4; McVey, 111.

81 Ephrem, *HNat* 15: 7-8; McVey, 146-47.

82 E.g., Ephrem, *HNat* 6: 3-4; 10; 12; 13: 13; 14: 11-13; 15: 7-8.

83 *HNat* 13: 13.

Ephrem's context, the taunts probably indicate contemporary Jewish-Christian hostilities.[84]

Sexual slander was a favored strategy in the rhetorical tropes of Greco-Roman invective.[85] Its use
against Christians was not only to ridicule the idea
of a virgin birth, but also to impugn the legitimacy
of the larger Christian community. Indeed, Ephrem's
verses dance between the sacred past and the lived
present. In his hymns, the calumny against Tamar,
Rahab, Ruth and Mary has been renewed. Now it
is calumny directed against the consecrated virgins
of the church, the women of his choir. For in these
hymns, Ephrem presents his virgin choir in typological relation to Mary: because Christ was born of a
virgin, virgins are exalted.

---

84   For the Jewish charges, see further Peter Schafer,
     Jesus in the Talmud (Princeton: Princeton University
     Press, 2007), 1-32; and more broadly, Jane Schaberg,
     The Illegitimacy of Jesus. For Ephrem's context, Shepa-
     rdson, *Anti-Judaism and Christian Orthodoxy*.

85   Jennifer Wright Knust, *Abandoned to Lust: Sexual
     Slander and Ancient Christianity* (New York: Colum-
     bia University Press, 2006); Valentina Arena, "Roman
     Oratorical Invective," in *A Companion to Roman Rheto-
     ric*, ed. William Dominik and Jon Hall (Malden, MA:
     Wiley-Blackwell, 2007), 149-60.

> Let chaste women praise that pure Mary.
> Since in their mother Eve their disgrace was great,
> Behold in Mary their sister their triumph was magnified.
> Blessed is He who shone forth from them![86]

Standing in Mary's place, however, the virgins also suffer her same injuries. Just as Mary's virginity had been maligned, so is theirs.

> You [O Christ] dwelt in Mary, but the unclean said falsely
> That the fetus was not Yours. Since You dwell now
> Within the chaste women, behold they are slandered
> As [if they were] pregnant. They slander the pregnant one
> And those who are not pregnant – a great atrocity![87]

The Nativity feast in Ephrem's verses vindicates the choice of these virgins, just as it had vindicated Mary and before her, the scandalous foremothers. All of these women suffered unjustly, and all are shown for their true worth in the light of Christ's birth. Thus these same hymns advocate not only the consecrated virgins of Ephrem's church (the choir), but also virginity itself as a vocation.

---

86 *HNat* 22: N23; McVey, 183.

87 *HNat* 12: 9.

Ephrem's defense of virginity in the Nativity hymns indicates the degree to which the Christian ideal of celibacy at first disrupted social order in the Roman east. However much monasticism would become a respected institution over the course of the following century, in Ephrem's own time the rise of ascetic piety was problematic in the eyes of many. Ephrem's *Hymns on the Nativity*, among their other accomplishments, provided a spirited defense for celibacy as a vocation to be enacted within the civic sphere. The consecrated virginity extolled in these hymns was not that of a remote or removed monastic life, lived separately from the civic world of families and the marketplace. Such a development had not yet become common in the eastern Mediterranean, although it was beginning to appear.[88] Rather, his choirs and their devotional life were set at the heart of the ecclesial community: in the very church building to which the Christian population came routinely for morning or evening prayers, for Sunday liturgies, feast days, and festivals.

Thus the subjectivity of Ephrem's Mary is complex, even multiple. She speaks sometimes in biblical character, bringing poignancy to the laconic gospel texts. Sometimes she is also the voice of the maligned

88   On the emergence of Syrian monasticism, see Sidney H. Griffith, "Asceticism in the Church of Syria: The Hermeneutics of Early Syrian Monasticism," in *Asceticism*, ed. Vincent Wimbush and Richard Valantasis (New York: Oxford University Press, 1995), 220-45.

choirs and virgins of the church, suffering slander for their devotional choices. She is also the voice of the persecuted orthodox (Nicene) church that Ephrem championed so fiercely: pure in her devotion to Christ, battered but unwavering amidst competing Christian factions, the beacon of true faith. Hers is the voice of biblical past and liturgical present, of the devoted individual and the ecclesial collective. She is at once unique, and shared: singular as subject yet available to all, in words sung by women's choirs, male chanters, and congregational response.

In Ephrem's *Hymns on the Nativity*, then, focus on the women of Christ's lineage allows him to establish crucial claims about canon and doctrine, both. His emphasis on the genealogies of Matthew and Luke carried with it an insistence on a biblical canon that included both the Old and New Testaments. In the cities of Nisibis and Edessa where he wrote, Ephrem championed a small Nicene community, strongly outnumbered by rival Christian groups who rejected such a scripture: Marcionites, Manicheans, Valentinians. He also strove against well-established Jewish communities, whose anti-Christian invective was in part their own claim to ownership of the Hebrew Bible. Again, focus on the scandalous women of Matthew's genealogy meant that Ephrem affirmed the physicality of Jesus' human lineage and birth. This allowed Ephrem a theological opposition to teachings that denigrated the sanctity of God's physical, material creation, such as these rival Christian groups taught. Moreover, Ephrem competed with large communities of Arian Christians. Celebration of the scandalous biblical women allowed him to claim that the Old Testament, including the messianic lineage, belonged to orthodox (Nicene) Christians. At the same time, he used the vindication of Mary to demonstrate the full divinity of the incarnate Lord, where Arians (like Jews, in Ephrem's view) would deny or undervalue it.[89]

The Nativity Feast itself was a recent institution when Ephrem wrote these hymns. It may well have been established as a means of counteracting Arian Christianity, allowing as it did an affirmation of Christ's full divinity through the exaltation of his incarnation.[90] As such, it provided a powerful stage upon which to mount a defense for consecrated virginity as a civic virtue. The context of a civic religious feast, the location of a liturgical celebration, and the performance of Ephrem's hymns by choirs of consecrated virgins were all aspects contributing to the profound social and cultural force of Ephrem's defense of celibacy in the service of the church con-

89   See especially Shepardson, *Anti-Judiasm and Christian Orthodoxy*, 21-68.

90   See Peter G. Cobb, "The History of the Christian Year," in *The Study of Liturgy*, ed. Cheslyn Jones, Geoffrey Wainwright, Edward Yarnold, and Paul Bradshaw, rev. ed. (New York: Oxford University Press, 1992), at p. 467.

gregation in its broadest sense. His celebration of women of holy scandal – of holy impudence – past and present, could also be heard as the summons for women's participation in the work of the church in the world.

A century and more later, Jacob of Serug's homily on Tamar was even more explicit in its depiction of the messianic lineage as driven by a "holy lust." He goes further than Ephrem, casting the salacious imagery even on the "righteous" foremothers Leah and Rachel. These "straightforward women of integrity," inflamed with the "fire" of divine love, competed to bear Jacob's sons. As Jacob told the story in solemn cadence, they had acted shamefully, "impudently," in ways "most hateful to chaste women," "like a prostitute," "like someone loving adultery." Ruth, too, Jacob intoned, had appeared to be a "wanton woman" when she crawled under Boaz's cloak. "She was not ashamed, chaste woman that she was, to seize hold of his legs," Jacob insisted. Again, he preached, "It was not harlotry in the case of these sincere women, but love for the blessed seed that incited them." Turning to Tamar, he stated emphatically: "Her action was (indeed) ugly, but her faith made it beautiful."[91]

---

91   Jacob of Serug, "On Tamar," vv. 73-157; ed. and trans. Sebastian P. Brock, "Jacob of Serugh's Verse Homily on Tamar (Gen. 38)," *Le Muséon* 115 (2002): 279-315, at 295-96.

What is striking about Ephrem and Jacob is not
only their emphasis on the physicality of these scandalous actions, but also the context of their presentations. These were hymns and homilies performed
in civic churches, in the public gatherings of men
and women. Yet no apologies are offered for the
improprieties of these stories. In both cases, there
were surely polemical motives. Jacob of Serug, writ-
ing a century and more after Ephrem, was no longer
fighting for a canon or creed. But he, like Ephrem,
struggled with competing Christologies in heated
crisis, in the debates that followed the Council of
Chalcedon in 451.[92] I would suggest that his homily
on Tamar is a similar response to theological con-
troversy. Jacob's spotlight on Jesus' physical genealogy and hence the physicality of his incarnation held
theological implications. It allowed him to empha-
size a fully human, fully divine savior in the midst
of a conflict that threatened distortion in one direc-
tion or the other. The stories of these biblical women
could make that claim with unequivocal force, and in
memorable terms.

---

92 Although eirenic and understated in his own presentation of the volatile Christological controversies
of his time, Jacob was a leading figure among the anti-
Chalcedonians. He is revered to this day among the
Syriac Orthodox Christians as one of their greatest
theologians.

2. THE VIRGIN MARY AND HER 'DAUGHTERS'

In Syriac Christianity, as for others, the Virgin Mary holds pride of place among biblical women and indeed, among female saints. Numerous hymns and homilies were dedicated to her, and she features prominently in countless other Syriac writings.[93] Different authors cast her figure in different ways, even when continuing themes which earlier theologians had set out (usually, Ephrem). In Jacob of Serug's verse homilies on Mary and on the Nativity, for example, Mary is a figure of formidable mind and powerful will.[94] As the Second Eve, she must undo the failures of her foremother to reconcile humankind once again with God. Although she was "a humble daughter of poor folk," she yet stood in stern confrontation with the "fiery Watcher," the Archangel Gabriel, determining the fate of all humanity.[95] For Jacob, Mary's agency is crucial. In his telling, it

93   On Mary in Syriac tradition, see Robert Murray, *Symbols of Church and Kingdom: A Study in Early Syriac Tradition*, 2nd ed. (Piscataway, NJ: Gorgias Press, 2004), 144-50, 329-35.

94   These are conveniently collected and translated in Mary Hansbury, *Jacob of Serug on the Mother of God* (Crestwood, NY: St. Vladimir's Seminary Press, 1998) and Thomas Kollamparampil, *Jacob of Serug, Select Festal Homilies* (Rome: Centre for Indian and Inter-Religious Studies, 1997).

95   Jacob of Serug, *On the Mother of God*, Hom. 1, Hansbury, p. 29.

was her discerning intellect that led her to question
the Archangel at length before deciding, of her own
free will, that she would agree to receive the incarnation. For Eve had once followed the Serpent's lead
without question, "in silence." In contrast, Mary received her divine messenger with sharp-minded and
probing voice: "By Eve's silence, [came] guilt and the
fouling of a name;/ by Mary's discourse, [came] life
and light with victory."[96]

A master storyteller, Jacob presents the exchange
between Mary and Gabriel as filled with suspense.
Mary's agreement was not preordained. Her words
were mighty: she had the power to stymie God's
plans, or to fulfill them. Here, he marveled, was the
measure of her beauty: she chose her course of her
own free will.[97]

In one of his festal homilies on the Nativity, Jacob
portrayed Mary's strength of will by suggesting her
mastery over the entire event of the holy conception.
Having made her choice, she gave her consent to Gabriel. But she would not allow the conception to pro-
ceed until she deemed herself ready. Jacob's depiction
of her preparations is at once exalted and humble.
For Mary sets to work like an earnest housewife pre-
paring her home for a royal visitor. She cleans, dusts,

96   Jacob of Serug, *On the Mother of God*, Hom. 1,
     Hansbury, p. 33.
97   Jacob of Serug, *On the Mother of God*, Hom. 1,
     Hansbury, at p. 25.

tidies up and repairs the house of her soul, sweeping away any unworthy thoughts, casting out any worthless sentiments, polishing up the shine of her virtues. She mends the damaged or worn parts, sets anything messy in order. She freshens, replenishes, and renews with sweet thoughts, good intentions, and reverence. She adorns and embellishes with piety, virtues, and prayer. As she works, she sings hymns of thanksgiving. When all is radiant and beautiful, she opens the door and invites her Lord to enter.[98] It is a poignant depiction, yet one that sets Mary's will once again as a mighty force:

> She answered to the watcher [Gabriel] with great love, 'Let your Lord come.
>
> Behold, I am prepared so that according to His will He might dwell within me.'
>
> … By her will she opened the door and then the King entered so that through free will the perfect seal might be honored.[99]

In Ephrem's Nativity hymns, Mary speaks only in monologues (her "lullabyes"). She sings directly to

98 Jacob of Serug, "On Nativity 1 (Festal Homily 1)," pp. 59-60, vv. 387-418. For discussion of this extraordinary passage, see S. A. Harvey, "Interior Decorating: Jacob of Serug on Mary's Preparation for the Incarnation," *Studia Patristica* 41, ed. F. Young, M. Edwards and P. Parvis (Leuven: Peeters, 2006), 23-28.

99 Jacob, "On Nativity 1 (Festal Homily 1)," vv. 411-18. See S.A. Harvey, "Interior Decorating."

Christ, and (by implication) to us, her congregation.
Jacob's homilies, however, set Mary in conversation
with others from her story: Gabriel, Joseph, Elizabeth, and the Magi are all depicted together with
Mary in verbal exchange and extended dialogue. For
both Ephrem and Jacob, Mary's character is best conveyed through her imagined speech, the voice they
each crafted with such care to portray the power of
her place in God's divine plan. In an interesting contrast, the East Syriac poet Narsai (5th century) presents Mary almost wholly through narrative, allowing
her only a few lines of speech in a verse homily of
some length (three lines in a homily of 507 lines!).[100]

As was his habit, Jacob of Serug drew widely in
his homilies on Mary from other hymns and homilies, utilizing strands from broader Syriac traditions.
Indeed, a number of anonymous Syriac dialogue
hymns survive to us that present Mary's conversa-
tions with these same biblical characters in similar terms.[101] In these hymns, Mary is canny, wise,
shrewd, and resourceful. Sung antiphonally between
male and female choirs, these dialogues can take the
tone of comic banter or of haunting drama.

In numerous hymns on the Annunciation, for example, Mary will not agree to accept the incarnation

100   Narsai, "A Homily on Our Lord's Birth from the
      Holy Virgin," ed. and trans. F. McLeod, *Patrologia Ori-
      entalis* 40.1 (1979): 38-69.

101   Conveniently collected in Brock, *Bride of Light*.

until she understands how it will take place. Gabriel is exasperated by her refusal to be silent and obedient. He complains: "The angelic hosts quake at [God's] word:/ the moment He has commanded, they do not answer back;/ how is it then that you are not afraid/ to query the thing which the Father has willed?"[102] But in pointed repartee, even the archangel is no match for Mary's intellectual agility.[103]

In the dialogue hymns, Mary's husband Joseph is by turns somber and angry, as he and Mary debate her pregnancy. His is the righteous voice of reason, hers the shining conviction of faith. He demands her silence; she declares her word of truth.[104] In a dialogue with the Magi, Mary suspects they have come to harm her newborn child. Courageous and resourceful, she spars with them with shrewd agility, while they flounder in frustration. She will not allow entry to her baby until she is convinced of their purpose.[105] In another hymn, she (and not Mary Magdalene) finds the empty tomb and implores the gardener –

---

102 Anon., "Mary and the Angel," trans. Brock, *Bride of Light*, 114.

103 Anon., "Mary and the Angel," trans. Brock, *Bride of Light*, 111-18; cp. Jacob of Serug, "On Nativity 1 (Festal Homily 1)," at vv. 155-382, Kollamparampil, at 49-59.

104 Anon., Joseph and Mary; trans. Brock, *Bride of Light*, 118-24; cp. Jacob of Serug, "On Nativity 1 (Festal Homily 1)," at vv. 555-762, Kollamparampil, at 67-75.

105 Anon., "Mary and the Magi," trans. Brock, *Bride of Light*, 125-32.

the resurrected Lord, whom she does not recognize –
to help her find the body. In the hymn, Christ as the
gardener tries to maintain his disguise until Mary's
purposeful badgering finally wears him out. In ex-
asperation he sings, "How you weary me with your
talk,/ how you vex me with what you say!"[106]

Syriac dialogue hymns often take a light-hearted,
even comic tone as they present biblical characters arguing or debating over many verses. In these
hymns, other biblical women match the quick-wit-
ted Mary who exasperates her dialogue partners. For
example, the Widow of Sarepta succeeds in harass-
ing the prophet Elijah to work the miracle of rain,
where heaven, earth, and even God himself had all
failed to move the stubborn prophet to action![107]

But here, too, in the antiphonal performance of
the dialogue hymns, the congregation had a role to
play. They were again not a passive audience. For the
soghyatha (dialogue hymns), as a form of madrashe
(doctrinal hymns), generally included a refrain punc-
tuating the stanzas. The refrains for these dialogues
were often the same, or very similar to one another:

> Praise to You, Lord, for at Your coming
> Sinners turned from their wickedness

106   Anon., "Mary and the Gardener," trans. Brock,
Bride of Light, 132-34.

107   Sebastian P. Brock, "A Syriac Verse Homily on Elijah and the Widow of Sarepta," *Le Muséon* 102 (1989):
93-113.

And entered into the protection of Eden and
the Garden
  Which is the holy church.[108]

By such prayers, the faithful were reminded time and
again that God's purpose was at work, even in the
unlikeliest of circumstances.

3. LAMENTING WOMEN

Greek literature enshrines a long and rich tradition of recalling Mary's lamentations for her son,
sung at the cross and then at the burial of Jesus.[109]
In Syriac, only one such lament is known to be ex-
tant.[110] An unedited homily by Jacob of Serug presents the theme of Mary at Golgotha, but its theme
is not lamentation so much as Christ's victory over
death.[111] Yet lamentation was very much a part of
the work that women's voices (and sometimes those

108 For example, in the dialogue hymns on Mary and
     Joseph, and Mary and the Magi; also on the Sinful
     Woman and Satan (see below, n. 132).

109 The classic study is Margaret Alexiou, *The Ritual
     Lament in Greek Tradition* (Cambridge: Cambridge
     University Press, 1974). See also Gail Holst-Warhaft,
     *Dangerous Voices: Women's Laments and Greek Litera-
     ture* (New York: Routledge, 1992).

110 Anon., "Mary at the Cross;" trans. Brock, *Bride of
     Light*, 108-10.

111 P. Mouterde, "Deux homelies inédites de Jacques
     de Sarug," *Mélanges de l'Université Saint Joseph* 26
     (1944/6): 1-36.

of men) offered in Syriac liturgy. Most often, these
laments appear as scenes that did not occur in the
biblical text of the story in which they are set. Yet
their crafting enables profound treatment of major
theological themes. Syriac writers cast these lamentations, fittingly, to honor beloved characters who
tragically died. Such was the ancient Mediterranean
heritage.[112] But they also used lament to account for
human life that is tragically lived, above all in the
recognition of human sin and folly. There is thus a
movement in these lamentations from mourning to
penitence: from grief at the finality of loss, to the
glimmer of hope that there can yet be a changed out-
come if people repent and change their lives.

Insofar as Syriac liturgical poetry was composed
for public, collective worship, it served as a vehicle
for moral formation towards a communal goal. It
worked to shape and mold faithful Christians, to
form virtuous, devoted citizens whose lives would
exemplify the truths their religion claimed. The con-
stancy with which Syriac hymns and verse homilies
presented their subjects through first-person speech
was a rhetorical strategy that served this purpose.
For in each instance, who was the subject of the
speaker/singer? Hymns and homilies presented biblical characters as types, mirrored images one of an-

---

112   E.g., Ann Suter, ed., *Lament: Studies in the Ancient
       Mediterranean and Beyond* (New York: Oxford Univer-
       sity Press, 2008).

other to reveal the unfolding of the salvation drama in its fullness. But they also presented them as types of moral virtue: models for Christians to follow, and to which they should conform, that would imprint true virtue upon the lives they lived. The subject here was not the unique, personal individual our contemporary society understands persons to be. Instead, it was the individual always as microcosm of the collective whole. Each biblical character explored through song and chant offered a model for the individual believer, and also for the church as a whole.[113] Ephrem's Mary, as noted above, was the unjustly maligned yet faithful believer; she was also the virgin choir, slandered in the public sphere yet bearing faithful witness to their Lord; she was also the Church, faithful Bride of her Heavenly Bridegroom, again persecuted and wronged but steadfast. It was the work of hymn and homily to mold the subjectivity of the believer into the form befitting the faithful one betrothed to Christ. The subject in each of these presentations became the liturgical subject: the individual in the form of the congregation as a collective, and in the person of its individual members. I would suggest that lamentation was a particularly effective instance of the liturgical formation of the faithful believer.

---

113   Crucial now to work on ancient notions of subjectivity is Christopher Gill, *The Structured Self in Hellenistic and Roman Thought* (New York: Oxford University Press, 2009).

Thus Jacob of Serug presents Eve in vivid grief at the murder of Abel, torn as to which of her two sons she should mourn.[114] She sings a double-lamentation, for her son Abel who is dead and also for her son Cain, now lost irrevocably in his tragic demise. Eve's voice provides the measure of human sorrow. She is not only stricken as the one who lost Paradise. She is also Eve, Mother of Life: her sorrow is the sorrow of all mortal beings in the face of death's constant presence. She is often recalled in Syriac liturgical poetry in binary opposition to Mary, the Second Eve. Sometimes this is a simple correspondence: from the one came death, from the other came life. But more often Eve is recalled as a tragic figure whose redemption is Mary's deed. She is the one whose debt Mary pays; the one bowed down whom Mary raises up. Like Adam, she waits among the dead to be restored to life.

In an anonymous hymn, the intimacy between Eve and Mary is extolled: "The Daughter gave support to her mother who had fallen,/ and because she had clothed herself in fig leaves of shame/ her daughter wove and gave her a garment of glory."[115] And in an-

---

114   Jacob of Serug, Hom. 149, "On Cain and Abel III [Eve's Lament]," Bedjan and Brock, vol. 5, 32-47. See J.B. Glenthøj, *Cain and Abel in Syriac and Greek Writers (4th – 6th Centuries)*, CSCO 567/ Sub. 95 (Leuven: Peeters, 1997).

115   Anon., "Hymns on Mary" 2: 9; trans. Brock, *Bride of Light*, 36.

other, both foreparents are summoned with compassion:

> The Virgin Vine gave forth the Cluster of grapes
> whose wine is sweet.
>   Both Adam and Eve who were mourning
>   received comfort in their grief,
>   having tasted of that Medicine of Life,
>   they received comfort in their grief.[116]

By such verses, Eve (like Adam) remains part of the human community, both in the grief of loss and death, and in the hope of joy to come.

The Joseph saga gains a poignant dimension by the addition of his sister Dinah to Syriac accounts of Joseph's reunion with his father Jacob, in Genesis 46. In a number of verse homilies and dialogue hymns, Dinah is present alongside Jacob through long nights as Joseph tells them of all he survived after the treachery of his brothers.[117] She is the one who summons him to tell his story, and the one who narrates in return the wretched grief of those who

---

116   Anon., "Hymns on Mary" 1: 14; trans. Brock, *Bride of Light*, 35.

117   Sebastian P. Brock, "Dinah in a Syriac Poem on Joseph," in *Semitic Studies in honour of Edward Ullendorff*, ed. Geoffrey Khan, Studies in Semitic Languages and Linguistics 47 (Leiden: Brill, 2005), 222-35; Kristian Heal, *Tradition and Transformation: Genesis 37 and 39 in Early Syriac Sources* (Ph.D. thesis, University of Birmingham 2006), 235-57.

loved Joseph and believed he had died. She cares for
the elderly Jacob when the emotion of the reunion
causes him to faint; she herself swoons with horror
as Joseph recounts his sufferings. Above all, she is
the lamenting woman who ceaselessly mourned the
loss of her brother through the many years of his ab-
sence. In her own sorrow during that long time, she
became the sorrow of all who grieved. She describes
her communal role to her brother, telling how instead of attending weddings,

> I would go to the graveyard and weep for you
> there, my brother.
> There was no newly departed in the vale of
> Hebron whose bier I did not escort
> As I lamented and wept because of you.
> At the beginning of all my laments, it was your
> person I would recall, Joseph.
> There was no limit to the way the Hittite women
> loved me,
> Thinking that it was for their departed that I
> was weeping, my brother.
> They would thank me – when it was for you
> I wept!
> And they said to our father, 'Dinah, your daugh-
> ter, Jacob, should be remembered
> For how much she weeps and laments together
> with us over our dead.
> Great is her love as she pours out her compas-
> sion: blessed is her father!'[118]

---

118   Ps.-Narsai IV, cited in Brock, "Dinah," 231.

With the depiction of Dinah's grief as the articulation of every grief in the community, we see something of civic life in antiquity: every life, every death belonged to the community as a whole. While Dinah insists her mourning was singular, yet the listener – like Dinah's neighbors in the story – recognizes the universal dimension of sorrow and loss.

Another lamenting woman appears in Jacob of Serug's homily on the Judgment of Solomon to the two harlots.[119] The mother of the living child sings bitter grief three times in this extraordinary homily. Her weeping begins when she mistakenly thinks her child has died. When she discovers the dead child is not hers, but that her own – still living – has been claimed by another, her milk and tears pour forth in agony. The fighting of the women brings the case before Solomon, who delivers his verdict to cut the child in two. In her anguished plea that the child's life might be spared, even to be raised by the wrong mother, the harlot's words take on a visceral, wrenching eloquence that breaks the heart of all who were present. Seeing the true mother thus revealed, Solomon's wisdom is acclaimed by all.

Perhaps most strikingly, in the hands of Syriac writers Sarah the wife of Abraham stood as the true

---

119   Jacob of Serug, Hom. 111, "On the Judgment of
      Solomon [On the Two Harlots]," Bedjan and Brock,
      vol. 4, 116-32; trans. Stephen A. Kaufman (Piscataway,
      NJ: Gorgias Press, 2008).

hero in the episode of Genesis 22, the sacrifice of
Isaac. She was the one whose response to God was
immediate, albeit shrouded with grief. While Abraham devised tricks and lies, first to Sarah and then to
Isaac, Sarah brought courage, wisdom, and strength
to the event. In the dialogue hymns and an anonymous verse homily, Abraham blusters his empty de-
ceits while Sarah discerns the truth with penetrating
yet agonized faith that God's intention must be true.
In another anonymous verse homily, after Abraham
has departed with Isaac for the mountain, Sarah
sings a lament for the death of her only son that
prefigures with searing clarity the grief of the Virgin
Mary at the cross.[120]

In an anonymous dialogue hymn on Abraham and
Sarah in Egypt (Genesis 12), the portrait of Sarah
in suffering lamentation reappears. Here Sarah is
titled "Daughter of the Poor." The title designates
her condition as one unjustly afflicted whose faith
is yet true, for in the story Abraham attempts to en-
sure their safety by offering Sarah to Pharoah for
marriage, pretending she is his sister. Abraham is
once again depicted as cowardly, deceitful, and un-
discerning. But Sarah remains steadfast in her faith
that God will deliver them from their trial. In agony

---

120   Sebastian P. Brock, "Genesis 22 in Syriac Tradi-
       tion," in *Mélanges D. Barthélemy* (*Orbis Biblicus et Ori-
       entalis* 38, 1981), 1-30; idem, "Two Verse Homilies on
       the Binding of Isaac."

she pleads with Abraham not to despise their love by passing her off to Pharaoh illegitimately. Stricken with grief, she is the suffering innocent as she prays for deliverance en route to wrongful marriage. As great is her faith, so dazzling is her beauty to the Egyptians, until the truth is revealed and Pharoah mourns his error.[121]

To the discerning listener, of course, a haunting refrain lies behind all these laments. For the harlot mother witnesses the rescue of the child she thought to be as good as dead from the executioner's sword, just as Dinah witnesses the return of the brother whose death she mourned without ceasing, and Sarah will witness not only the preservation of her rightful marriage (with its fruit, her son Isaac) but also the return of Isaac still living from Mount Moriah. Even Eve's lament would be turned from sorrow to joy, once she was raised up by her daughter's living hand. Each of these laments, sung in the cadenced dignity of the liturgical cycle, held within it the promise of life again. If the congregation heard Mary's voice at the tomb of her Son in each of these lamentations, they also knew where the ending of the story would lead. Indeed, did not every mother, every sister, every daughter, every spouse who lost their

---

121   Sebastian P. Brock and Simon A. Hopkins, "A Verse Homily on Abraham and Sarah in Egypt: Syriac Original with Early Arabic Translation," *Le Muséon* 105 (1992): 87-146.

loved one sing in Mary's voice? Just as Ephrem had titled Mary by all these relations when he named her relation to Christ – Mother, Daughter, Sister, Bride – so, too, did every believer stand in her place, at the cross, at the tomb, and at the Resurrection.[122]

4. HOLY TEARS: THE SINFUL WOMAN

That the tears of lament should transform to the tears of penance we might suspect from Eve's double lament for her two sons, one dead and one still living. And indeed, in the unending tears that stream from the eyes of the Sinful Woman at the feet of Christ, Syriac writers found the figure to weave the disparate threads together.[123] In her, lamentation was for the death of the soul, not of the body. By her tears, as if from the very baptismal font itself, new life was born. Syriac liturgical prayers as early as the fourth century call for the individual believer to pray with penitent tears following her model.[124]

Apart from the Virgin Mary, there was perhaps no woman of the Bible more loved by Syriac poets than the Sinful Woman who came to the house of Simon

122   Ephrem, *HNat* 11: 2, 16: 9.

123   Consider the suggestive contributions in Kimberley Christine Patton and John Stratton Hawley, *Holy Tears: Weeping in the Religious Imagination* (Princeton: Princeton University Press, 2005).

124   J. Gribomont, "La Tradition Liturgique des Hymnes Pascales de S. Éphrem," *Parole de l'Orient* 4 (1973): 191-246, at p. 219.

the Pharisee to wash the feet of Christ with her
tears, dry them with her hair, and anoint them with
fine oil. Late antique Syriac authors leave her unnamed and unidentified, just as the gospel account in
Luke 7:37 ("a woman of the city, who was a sinner").
While they freely intermingled the gospel accounts
from Matthew, Mark, and Luke, they followed Luke
most often.[125] And although they sometimes saw her
actions echoed in those of Mary Magdalene or Mary
of Bethany, they preferred to keep these women as
separate figures, with different stories to tell.

A sizeable number of verse homilies and dialogue poems survive in Syriac devoted to this biblical woman.[126] She was often contrasted with Simon
the Pharisee, in multiple polarities: her silence and
his speech, her fasting and his feast, her actions and
his inaction, her understanding and his mispercep-
tion, her certainty and his doubt.[127] Most influential
was an anonymous verse homily, wrongly attributed

---

125   Mt 26:6-13, Mk 14:3-9, Lk 7:36-50.

126   The available texts and translations are listed in
S.A. Harvey, "Why the Perfume Mattered: The Sinful
Woman in Syriac Exegetical Tradition," *In Dominico
Eloquio/ In Lordly Eloquence: Essays on Patristic Exegesis
in Honor of Robert Wilken*, ed. P. Blowers, A. Christ-
man, D. Hunter, and R. Darling Young (Grand Rapids,
MI: Eerdmans, 2001), 69-89.

127   For example, in Ephrem's *Homily on Our Lord*, sec.
42-48; trans. Amar and Mathews, *St. Ephrem: Prose
Works*, 273-332, at 316-24.

to Ephrem, which provided the extensive narrative
that gave the Woman her own story and her own
voice.[128] As with the Virgin Mary, she was depicted
as a woman of self-directed agency. As with Tamar
or Ruth, a holy impudence compelled her. She chose
her way and proceeded. Neither pious men nor the
wiles of Satan turned her from her course. In this
story, every man she meets is an obstacle, until she
arrives at the holy feet of her Lord.

Some of the poets follow the gospel model and
preserve this Woman's silence, allowing her tears
and her actions to function as speech. But the homily wrongly attributed to Ephrem grants her a voice
that will be echoed in two dialogue hymns between
the Woman and Satan. In the homily she speaks
first an extensive lament of remorse and conversion
while stripping off the garments and jewels of harlotry, exchanging them for the sackcloth and ashes
of penance.[129] Then follows the dialogue that sets
her in fierce debate with the earnest Perfume Seller,
from whom she must obtain the fine ointment but
who doubts her cause. Next is the dispute with a dis-

128 Ephrem (?), Sermon 4, "On the Sinful Woman,"
     ed. Edmund Beck, *Des Heiligen Ephraem des Syrers,
     Sermones* II, CSCO 311/ Scr. Syr. 134 (1970), 78-91;
     trans. idem, CSCO 312/ Scr. Syr. 135, 99-109; English
     trans. by John Gwynn, NPNF 13, 336-41.

129 J.M. Sauget, "Une homélie syriaque sur la pécher-
     esse attribuée à un évêque Jean," *Parole de l'Orient* 6/7
     (1975/6): 159-94.

gruntled Satan in the guise of a spurned lover who seeks to woo her back. Finally comes the dialogue with the scandalized Simon, the Pharisee who seeks to prevent her entrance into his house and into the presence of Christ, by any and every means.[130] Finally, driven by the power of her love alone, she arrives at His feet.

From the Syriac original, this account of the Sinful Woman spread into Greek and then Latin, widely influencing medieval dramas on the story.[131] The episode of her encounter with the Perfume Seller proved one of the most popular, receiving notable treatment in a brilliant Greek *kontankion* by Romanos the Melodist in the sixth century,[132] and in a

---

130   Sebastian P. Brock, "The Sinful Woman and Satan: Two Syriac Dialogue Poems," *Oriens Christianus* 72 (1988): 21-62.

131   A.C. Mahr, *Relations of Passion Plays to St. Ephrem the Syrian* (Columbus, OH: Wartburg, 1942); idem, *The Cyprus Passion Cycle* (Notre Dame, IN: University of Notre Dame Press, 1947), 36-38, 50-52.

132   Romanos, Melodos, "On the Sinful Woman," ed. J. Grosdidier de Matons, *Romanos le Mélode, Hymnes*, Sources Chrétiennes 114 (Paris: Cerf, 1965), vol. 2, 20-43. Two fine English translations are available: R. Schork, *Sacred Song from the Byzantine Pulpit* (Gainsville, FL: University of Florida Press, 1995), 77-85; and Ephrem Lash, *St. Romanos the Melodist, Kontakia On the Life of Christ* (San Francisco: HarperCollins, 1995), 75-84.

much loved Syriac hymn still sung today by Syriac
Orthodox Christians.

A number of the homilies cast the story in terms
of ritual meanings. Tears (water), kisses (venera-
tion), and perfumed ointment (anointment) are
highlighted with overt liturgical imagery, and the
Woman is portrayed in priestly terms. Her tears are
her baptismal waters, her kisses and hair her offer-
ings, and she herself the one who makes the ritual
oblation.[133] She is priest and penitent: "in place of
the priest, I myself make the offering to You."[134] To
Ephrem, she surpassed whatever efficacy religious
structures provided: "that sinful woman ... came to
God, not to priests, to forgive her debts."[135] To Jacob
of Serug, she was as "impudently bold" as Tamar the
daughter-in-law of Judah had been, transformed by
love that burned so fiercely she became at once sacri-
ficer and sacrificed.[136]

These hymns and homilies place heavy stress on
the Woman's capacity to make the decision to change
her life, and then to enact her purpose. No heavenly

133   F. Graffin, "Homélies anonymes du VIe siècle: Ho-
      mélies sur la pécheresse I, II, III," *Patrologia Orientalis*
      41 (Turnhout: Brepols, 1984): 449-527.

134   Graffin, Anonymous Homily 1, sec. 23, *Patrologia
      Orientalis* 41: 463.

135   Ephrem, *Homily on Our Lord* 46.1; trans. Amar
      and Matthews, 322.

136   S.A. Harvey, "Bride of Blood, Bride of Light," at
      200-2.

messengers arrive to help her choice or to guide her way; no human figure offers encouragement or hope. Indeed, every character added to the story represents an obstacle. In the dialogues with the Perfume Seller or Simon the Pharisee we hear the suffocating burdens of public reputations, social conventions, and respectable behavior. In the dialogues with Satan or the monologue with herself, we hear the internal battles of the divided self, assaulted by doubts, hesitation, worry, anxiety, and fear. And yet, in each of these encounters (and in each of the texts) the Sinful Woman triumphs over her past, her sins, her detractors, and herself, by her own will and conviction. The healing strength of Christ's forgiveness happens only once she has arrived at her goal: kneeling at his feet. Her arrival is her own doing.

The Sinful Woman was arguably the single most influential female figure in the ancient Syriac Christian imagination. Her gender was inseparably part of the story's power, for it carried the symbolic weight of the polarities of sex and virginity, embodiment and immateriality, female (weakness) and male (strength). Biblical men were also held up as images of conversion and penance: notably the Prodigal Son of Luke 15:11-32 and the Penitent Thief of Luke 23:39-43. Yet the Sinful Woman remains the enduring image of penitence and grace for Syriac writers. It is in her guise, molded to her model, in the form of her type, that Syriac poets urge every Christian to stand. The liturgical self, properly fashioned, is the penitent self.[137] Its truth is declared and its healing received, in the flow of holy tears that water its Life.

5. BIBLICAL WOMEN AS TYPES: THE WORK OF TYPOLOGY

The women of the gospels beyond those already cited received extensive attention in Syriac hymns and homilies. Named or (more often) unnamed in the New Testament, their figures gained renown in Christian tradition. They became types, models, for virtues and for the life of faith.

In Ephrem's *Hymns on Virginity* 26, for example, the New Testament women are intermingled with their Old Testament foremothers, exalted as brides of Christ, and thereby summoned as models of the church: Mary, Eve, Martha, Mary of Bethany, Sarah, the Sinful Woman, the Woman who called out the blessing (Lk 11:27-8), the Hemorrhaging Woman, the Widow with her two coins, the Canaanite Woman, the Widow of Nain, Jairus' Daughter, the Mother of the Sons of Zebedee (Mt 20:20-28), and the Wife of Pilate (Mt 27:19).[138] These Ephrem calls

137   Compare Derek Krueger, "Romanos the Melodist and the Christian Self in Early Byzantium," *Proceedings of the 21st International Congress of Byzantine Studies*, ed. E. Jeffreys and F.K. Haarer (Aldershot: Ashgate, 2006), 255-74.

138   Ephrem, *HVirg* 26; McVey, 376-81.

"the daughters of the innocent Eve,"[139] renaming the Virgin Mary according to her primordial mother and thereby tying together all women in their redeemed identities. The hymn closes with a magnificent blessing, in which these women are exalted as the Church herself, the Bride of Christ. Because they were thus joined to Christ, so was every woman:

> Blessed, then, are all of you, O chaste women,
> The church that was joined [in marriage] to the Son.
> It is a wonder how much the Holy One condescended
> So that women might be joined [in marriage] with honor.
> They received from His bounty, and they gave to Him and nourished Him.
> From His gift they reached out to Him and satisfied Him.
> He gave us a refined symbol in His intimacy.
> Glory to His purity![140]

Upheld collectively, each of these women is remembered as one with her own story of encounter with Christ. Each of those encounters is revelatory as a type for the individual believer and also for the Church as Bride of Christ.

Each of these women offered a model. In their variation, however, they were also seen as types one

139   *HVirg* 26: 1.
140   *HVirg* 26: 16; McVey, 381.

of another. Just as every true devotee might become
maligned and persecuted; or every lamentation
might mirror Mary's; or every encounter with Christ
promised resurrection, so the women of the Bible,
clustered in their groups of related stories, could be
interchanged one for another in their types of faith
and witness.

In the anonymous dialogue hymn on Sarah and
Abraham in Egypt, for example, Sarah is titled
"Daughter of the Poor," an epithet often applied by
Syriac writers to the Virgin Mary. The sharing of
titles – indeed, perhaps the transferability of titles
– was a common feature of Syriac poetry. By this de-
vice, perhaps we may understand something further
about typology in Syriac thought.

In a passage from a festal homily on the Nativity,
Jacob of Serug speaks of the feast as that occasion
when the Redeemer invites the Despised Woman
to enter his celebration. Who is she? A series of unnamed figures follow, as one by one Christ takes and
lifts up the Barren Woman, the Humiliated Woman,
the Sorrowful Woman, the Lamenting Woman, the
Enslaved Woman, the Woman who was Persecuted,
and the Imprisoned Woman, each now freed of her
suffering.[141] The passage is an arresting example of
early Syriac typology. It evokes Isaiah 54, where
God's redemption of the barren and repudiated

---

141   Jacob of Serug, "On Nativity 1 (Festal Homily 1),"
      Kollamparampil, 41-93.

wife is promised. It echoes Ezekiel 16 and the allegory of God's rescue of Israel, the disobedient harlot. It alludes to Galatians 4:22-31, the allegory of Hagar and Sarah as the enslaved and free women, foreshadowing the Synagogue and the Church. Its list of titled but unnamed women offers a powerful typological cluster of female figures who, in other Christian contexts, were identified with the Church as the disgraced and then redeemed Bride of Christ. The imagery was closely tied with anti-Jewish invective in which redemption is the rescue of the polluted Church from her imprisonment by unfaithful Zion.[142]

The titles in Jacob's list for the Disgraced Woman, in turn, appear attached to other biblical women elsewhere, whether in Jacob's homilies or other Syriac liturgical poetry. Eve is often titled as the woman whose bent or bowed head is raised by Mary at the

---

142   On the Church as Bride in Syriac tradition, and this particular clustering of images, see Robert Murray, *Symbols of Church and Kingdom: A Study in Early Syriac Tradition*, 2nd ed. (Piscataway, NJ: Gorgias Press, 2004), 131-42. There is an important Jewish development of this imagery, identifying the barren and redeemed woman with Sarah, as an allegory for Israel as the Bride of God. See Ophir Münz-Manor, "All About Sarah: Questions of Gender in Yannai's Poems on Sarah's (and Abraham's) Barrenness," *Prooftexts* 26 (2006): 344-74, esp. 346-51.

Nativity.[143] The title of Barren Woman is often applied to Elizabeth, Mary's kinswoman, and also to Sarah, Rachel, Rebecca, and Hannah, the Old Testament mothers of the messianic lineage.[144] The term Humiliated Woman is used for Tamar, the daughter-in-law of Judah (Genesis 38).[145] Similarly, Susanna (Dan. 13 LXX) is the Persecuted Woman; or she, like Sarah in Egypt (Gen 12), may also be the Humiliated One.[146] New Testament women also carried these titles. The Sinful Woman of Luke 7:36-52 is poetically styled the Sorrowful or Lamenting Woman (another title for Mary, at the cross), and also as the woman enslaved to Satan, rescued by her Bridegroom;[147] the Samaritan Woman of John 4 is the Reviled Woman,[148] or, with the Ca-

---

143   Jacob of Serug, *On the Mother of God*, Homily 3, Hansbury, at p. 82; Anonymous Hymns on Mary 2: 7, Brock, *Bride of Light*, 36; Anonymous Soghitha 2: 19, Brock, *Bride of Light*, 77.

144   For Elizabeth, e.g., Ephrem, *HVirg* 15: 1, 22: 14; *HNat* 2: 20, 6: 16, 21: 16-18; compare Jacob of Serug, *On the Mother of God*, Homily 2, Hansbury, 48, 52 (Elizabeth as the Sterile One).

145   E.g. Ephrem, *HNat* 9; Jacob of Serug, "On Tamar," l.205.

146   Ephrem, *HVirg* 22.

147   Ephrem, *HVirg* 35: 5-7; Brock, "The Sinful Woman and Satan"; Jacob of Serug, Hom. 51, "On the Sinful Woman."

148   Ephrem, *HVirg* 22: 9.

naanite Woman (Mt 15:21-28, Mk 7:24-30), one imprisoned amidst the idolatry of the heathen. The Hemorrhaging Woman (Mk 5:25-34 and parallels) would also be the Despised One, or the Humiliated One.[149]

For such biblical women, these titles carried a different sense of sacred narrative than that of the allegorical Church as Bride. They are for the most part examples of the innocent and faithful woman, wrongly accused, who suffers heroically yet unjustly – biblical women as types of Christ himself;[150] or they fit the paradigm of the Sinful Woman or the Samaritan Woman, as women whose redemption from their witting life of sin provides the most powerful measure of the salvific love of Christ.[151] These biblical figures are staples of late antique Syriac liturgical poetry both homiletic and hymnographic, their titles and their stories deeply familiar to the late antique church-goer. Such a passage, then, listing multiple biblical figures by titles rather than names, served to instruct the congregation in multiple ways. It suggested multiple stories by means of poetically

---

149 Compare Ephrem, *HVirg* 26 and 34.

150 Catherine Brown Tkacz, "Women as types of Christ: Susanna and Jephthah's Daughter," *Gregorianum* 85 (2004): 278-311; eadem, "'Here Am I, Lord' – Preaching Jephthah's Daughter as a Type of Christ," *The Downside Review* 434 (2006): 21-32.

151 E.g., Ephrem, *HVirg* 22, 26, 34; see Harvey, "Spoken Words, Voiced Silence."

employed titles, identified with but not exclusively owned by various biblical figures. Typological titles could thus open a variety of typologies, linking and suggesting different clusters of characters, stories, and models for faith.[152]

For Syriac poets, these titles provided the framework on which the entire salvation drama stood, enacted across the course of human history. Thus in one anonymous dialogue hymn, Mary sings as she calls to summon Eve forth from the place of the dead:

> Let Eve, our aged mother, now hear
> And come as I speak;
> Let her head, once bowed down in her naked state

---

152   On the ancient love for lists of titles, see Robert Murray, "Some Rhetorical Patterns in Early Syriac Literature," in *A Tribute to Arthur Vööbus: Studies in Early Christian Literature and its Environment, primarily in the Syrian East*, ed. R. H. Fischer (Chicago: Lutheran School of Theology at Chicago, 1977), 109-31. For the important tradition of listing biblical women and women saints in east Syriac liturgy, see J. M. Fiey, "Diptyques Nestoriens du XIVe siècle," *Analecta Bollandiana* 81 (1963): 371-413; idem, "Une hymne nestorienne sur les saintes femmes," *Analecta Bollandiana* 84 (1966): 77-110. A similar practice exists in the west Syriac liturgy, with the Book of Life. See R.H. Connolly, "The Book of Life," *Journal of Theological Studies* 13 (1912): 580-94; Andrew Palmer, "The Book of Life in the Syriac Liturgy: An Instrument of Social and Spiritual Survival," *The Harp* 4 (1991): 161-71.

> In the Garden, be raised up.
> Let her reveal her face and sing to You, [O Lord]
> For shamefacedness has passed away in You;
> Let her hear the message full of peace,
> For her daughter has repaid her debt.[153]

Because of Mary, Eve was called to sing her joy, "full of peace," because her debt was finished. Ultimately, in the eyes of Syriac poets, every Christian was called just so: to sing their praise for their Creator and Savior. In Jacob of Serug's festal homilies, he delights to name the figures of the gospel stories whose types had their counterparts in the ordinary lives of the Christian congregation. Because of their part in the saving story, each counterpart was called to take their place in the liturgical celebration. In cascades of glory, he calls them forth. Because Christ was the Ancient of Days, the elderly are to come. Because God became a child, the children should come. Because of his mother, mothers must come with their husbands. Because Christ was a babe held in arms, babies are brought by their parents and anointed in blessing. In these roll calls of the congregation, he joyfully nods to the women's choir: "A virgin conceived you, and so let the company of virgins be aroused [in song];/ let them stir up praise with wonder to your Father on

---

153 Anon., Soghitha 2: 19-20; Brock, *Bride of Light*, 77-78.

account of You [O Christ]."[154] In the end, because
Christ became human, everyone is called to join the
throng: "You became one of us and behold You are
ours while You are our Lord,/ and anyone who seeks
to speak of your story is entitled to do so."[155]

It is here, in the liturgical offering of the gathered
community in its entirety, that Jacob sees the work
of salvation underway. The women's choirs have
their place and purpose precisely because of this
typological ordering of the church community. According to Jacob, the instructional capacity of these
choirs was twofold. On the one hand, the content of
their hymns proclaimed the fundamental teachings
of the church. For when Ephrem had established
them, Jacob intoned, he had "admonished them …
to make their chants instructive melodies."[156] On the
other hand, their singing offered a series of typological models that imaged the salvation drama from the
Old Testament to the New.

Jacob laid forth the types in turn. First Moses had
summoned the Hebrew women to sing at the cross-
ing of the Red Sea, addressing them: "You passed
through the sea with brothers and fathers;/…You
witnessed terrors and wonders with your husbands;/ with them make a joyful sound to God

---

154   Jacob of Serug "On the Nativity 3 (Festal Homily
      3)," vv. 27-28, trans. Kollamparampil, p. 112.

155   Ibid, vv. 35-36.

156   Jacob of Serug, On Ephrem, 114, Amar, p. 53.

Almighty with your hosannas."[157] So Ephrem had established the women's choirs, in Jacob's telling, for they too had been saved from terror just as the men, but now through the holy waters of baptism. Even further, just as the font, so, too, the Eucharist: for the same baptism, the same bread and the same wine were offered to every Christian, male and female. Thus women as well as men must sing God's glory. Jacob imagines Ephrem addressing the women as he invited them to become a choir:

> You put on glory from the midst of the waters
> like your brothers;
> Render thanks with a loud voice like them also.
> You have partaken of a single forgiving body
> with your brothers,
> And from a single cup of new life you have been
> refreshed.
> A single salvation was yours and theirs (alike);
> why then
> Have you not learned to sing praise with a loud
> voice?[158]

Above all, Jacob sings, Eve had closed the mouth of women, but Mary their sister had opened it again — and opened it to sing forth with praise.

> Until now, your gender [lit. "side"] was brought
> low because of Eve;

157   Jacob of Serug, "On Ephrem," 82-83, Amar, p. 45.

158   Jacob of Serug, "On Ephrem," 105-7, Amar, p. 51.

But from now on, it is restored by Mary to sing
Alleluia!

...

Uncover your faces to sing praise without shame
To the One who granted you freedom of speech
by his birth.[159]

The work of the women's choirs was thus, according
to Jacob, a continual enactment of the work of salvation for humankind. They were types of the biblical women whose stories they sang, and types of the
Church as the collective embodiment of all believ-
ers. Their presence and their voices ensured that the
salvation drama was told and re-told in its totality.
It was a story that could not be told without them –
neither without the women who had been there as
God's purpose unfolded through sacred and human
time, nor without the women whose voices contin-
ued their presence in sacred song. Women's stories
fulfilled the Story. Women's voices proclaimed their
memory and their truth. In Syriac liturgy, biblical
women and women's choirs offered singular witness
to the salvation proclaimed for all.

---

159   Jacob of Serug, "On Ephrem," 111-13, Amar, p. 53.

The Père Marquette Lectures in Theology

1985 *From Vision to Legislation:*
   From the Council to a Code of Laws
     Ladislas M. Orsy, SJ
1986 *Revelation and Violence:*
   A Study in Contextualization
     Walter Brueggemann
1987 *Nova et Vetera:*
   The Theology of Tradition in American Catholicism
     Gerald Fogarty
1988 *The Christian Understanding of Freedom and the*
   History of Freedom in the Modern Era: The Meeting and
   Confrontation between Christianity and the Modern Era
   in a Postmodern Situation
     Walter Kasper
1989 *Moral Absolutes:*
   Catholic Tradition, Current Trends, and the Truth
     William F. May
1990 *Is Mark's Gospel a Life of Jesus?*
   The Question of Genre
     Adela Yarbro Collins
1991 *Faith, History and Cultures:*
   Stability and Change in Church Teachings
     Walter H. Principe, CSB
1992 *Universe and Creed*
     Stanley L. Jaki
1993 *The Resurrection of Jesus Christ:*
   Some Contemporary Issues
     Gerald G. O'Collins, SJ
1994 *Seeking God in Contemporary Culture*
     Most Reverend Rembert G. Weakland, OSB
1995 *The Book of Proverbs and Our Search for Wisdom*
     Richard J. Clifford, SJ
1996 *Orthodox and Catholic Sister Churches:*
   East Is West and West Is East
     Michael A. Fahey, SJ

ABOUT THE PÈRE MARQUETTE LECTURE SERIES

The Annual Père Marquette Lecture Series began at Marquette University in the Spring of 1969. Ideal for classroom use, library additions, or private collections, the Père Marquette Lecture Series has received international acceptance by scholars, universities, and libraries. Hardbound in blue cloth with gold stamped covers. Uniform style and price ($15 each). Some reprints with soft covers. Regular reprinting keeps all volumes available. Ordering information (purchase orders, checks, and major credit cards accepted):

Marquette University Press
Order Toll-Free (800) 247-6553 fax: (419) 281 6883
Order directly online: www.marquette.edu/mupress/
Editorial Address:
Dr. Andrew Tallon, Director
Marquette University Press
Box 3141
Milwaukee WI 53201-3141
phone: (414) 288-1564 fax: (414) 288-7813
email: andrew.tallon@marquette.edu
web: www.marquette.edu/mupress/

www.marquette.edu/mupress/
ISBN-13: 978- 0-87462-590-5
ISBN-10: 0-87462-590-4

9 780874 625905   5 1 5 0 0